The
Male Animal

A NEW COMEDY

By
James Thurber
and
Elliott Nugent

SAMUEL FRENCH, INC.
45 WEST 25TH STREET   NEW YORK 10010
7623 SUNSET BOULEVARD   HOLLYWOOD 90046
LONDON   *TORONTO*

SYNOPSIS OF SCENES

TIME: The present.

SCENE: The living room in the house of Professor Thomas
Turner, in a mid-western university town.

ACT I

Late fall. A Friday evening.

ACT II

SCENE 1. The following day, after lunch.
SCENE 2. Three hours later.

ACT III

Two days later, noon.

Program of the first performance of "THE MALE ANIMAL" as produced at the Cort Theatre, New York.

HERMAN SHUMLIN

PRESENTS

THE MALE ANIMAL

BY

JAMES THURBER AND ELLIOTT NUGENT

WITH

ELLIOTT NUGENT

STAGED BY MR. SHUMLIN
SETTING DESIGNED BY ALINE BERNSTEIN
COSTUMES SUPERVISED BY EMELINE CLARK ROCHE

CAST

(IN ORDER OF THEIR APPEARANCE)

CLEOTA	Played by	*Amanda Randolph*
ELLEN TURNER	" "	*Ruth Matteson*
TOMMY TURNER	" "	*Elliott Nugent*
PATRICIA STANLEY	" "	*Gene Tierney*
WALLY MYERS	" "	*Don De Fore*
DEAN FREDERICK DAMON	" "	*Ivan Simpson*
MICHAEL BARNES	" "	*Robert Scott*
JOE FERGUSON	" "	*Leon Ames*
MRS. BLANCHE DAMON	" "	*Minna Phillips*
ED KELLER	" "	*Matt Briggs*
MYRTLE KELLER	" "	*Regina Wallace*
"NUTSY" MILLER	" "	*Richard Beckhard*
NEWSPAPER REPORTER	" "	*John Boruff*

THE MALE ANIMAL

Comedy in three acts by James Thurber and Elliott Nugent, revived by the New York City Theatre Company at the City Center, April 30, 1952.

CAST OF CHARACTERS

CLEOTA	Eulabelle Moore
ELLEN TURNER	Martha Scott
TOMMY TURNER	Elliott Nugent
PATRICIA STANLEY	Nancy Nugent
WALLY MYERS	Charles Boaz
DEAN FREDERICK DAMON	Halliwell Hobbes
MICHAEL BARNES	John Gerstad
JOE FERGUSON	Robert Preston
MRS. BLANCHE DAMON	Ruth McDevitt
ED KELLER	Matt Briggs
MYRTLE KELLER	Regina Wallace
"NUTSY" MILLER	Billy James
NEWSPAPER REPORTER	Peter Harris

Time, 1940; the living room in the house of Prof. Thomas Turner in a midwestern university town. Act I. — Late Fall; a Friday evening. Act II. — Scene 1 — The following day; after lunch. Scene 2 — Three hours later. Act III. — Two days later; noon.

Staged by Michael Gordon; set by Melville Bourne; costumes by Noel Taylor; production stage manager, Billy Matthews.

"The Male Animal" was first produced by Herman Shumlin, January 9, 1940. The revival, scheduled for two weeks at the City Center, was so successful that John Golden took over the management for a commercial run at the Music Box Theatre.

STORY OF THE PLAY

A smash hit in New York City at the Cort Theatre as produced by Herman Shumlin with Elliott Nugent in the leading role. Tommy Turner has been married for ten years to Ellen, and he is quietly settled in a nice comfortable teaching job at Mid-Western University. But this is the week-end of the Michigan game, and Joe Ferguson, who was the greatest football hero Mid-Western ever had, comes to town, and of course, sees Ellen to whom he used to be sort of unofficially engaged. In addition to this slight upset in Tommy's life, he is brought into an academic controversy when Michael Barnes, a young college intellectual, writes an article for the literary magazine in which he calls the board of trustees "fascists!" Tommy, because he wants to read a letter to his composition class written by Vanzetti is about to have to join the ranks of the martyrs who got fired because the trustees are shouting "Red!" so loud they can't hear an idea tinkle. Ellen tries to dissuade Tommy from reading the letter, and this coupled with Joe's presence forces Tommy to ask her to go with Joe and leave him to his books and his principles. Eventually Tommy challenges Joe to fisticuffs after he has fortified himself with the proper courage. Also, he refuses to deny that he will read the Vanzetti letter and decides to stand on his principle of the freedom of ideas and the right to teach the young to think. Ellen now sees that he is a pretty good example of the male animal, and stands up with him.

If you are planning to produce THE MALE ANIMAL kindly note that we cannot authorize you to use in your production the following songs :—

WHO

HAPPY BIRTHDAY

OHIO STATE JELLOBALAD

These particular songs are not essential to the play and we would suggest that you substitute suitable music for them.

SAMUEL FRENCH

ACT ONE

SCENE: *The living room of a pleasant, inexpensive little house. There is no distinction of architectural design, but someone with natural good taste has managed to make it look attractive and liveable on a very modest budget. There are some good prints on the walls. The hangings are cheerful, and the furniture, picked up through various bargains and inheritances, goes together to make a pleasing, informal atmosphere.*

The front door, opening onto a porch, is upstage Left, the outer wall jogging into the room for a few feet. The inside of this outer wall is lined with book-shelves which continue around the corner to the fireplace in the Left wall. Below this fireplace is a stand with a radio-phonograph. In the Center of the rear wall, a bay window with window seat. This corner is used by the Turner family as a casual depository for visitors' hats and coats, although they have also a coat-rail just inside the front door. In front of the bay window, a long table backs a comfortable sofa facing front. To the Right of the bay window are more book-shelves, a small landing, and a stairway running up and off Right. In the corner below the stair near the dining room door, a table up Right against stairs has been prepared today to serve as a temporary bar, with a tray, cocktail shaker, and two or three bottles and glasses. In the Right wall, two doors, the upper one leading to the dining room, the lower one to another porch and back yard. There are two small

3

settees, one down Right, the other down Left near the fireplace. An arm-chair Right Center, a couple of small end or coffee tables, and one or two straight chairs complete the furnishings of the room. There are two or three vases of flowers, and the books and magazines which frequently litter this room have been put tidily away.

PHONE: Ring. Ring. Ring.

At the rise of the Curtain, the phone on table Right Center behind sofa is ringing. CLEOTA, *a colored maid, enters from the dining room Right and answers it.*

CLEOTA. Professah Turner's res-i-dence— Who?— You got de wrong numbah— Who?— What you say?— Oh, Mistah *Turner!* No, he ain't heah. He jus' went out to buy some likkah— Who is dis callin'? Yessuh. Yessuh. Ah doan' get dat, but Ah'll tell him Doctah Damon. Ah say Ah'll tell him. [*Hangs up; starts for dining room.*]

ELLEN'S VOICE. [*Off upstairs.*] Who was it, Cleota?

CLEOTA. It was Doctah Damon. [*Crossing to stair landing and looking upstairs.*] He say he comin' ovah to see Mistah Turner or Mistah Turner come over to see him, or sumpin'. [*Turns on LIGHTS from wall switch Left of dining room door.*]

[*LIGHT cue # 1.*]

ELLEN. [*Appearing on stairs.*] What was that again, Cleota? [*She crosses down Left toward coffee table. She is an extremely pretty young woman about twenty-nine or thirty. Quick of speech and movement she has a ready smile and a sweetness of personality that warms the room. She is completely feminine and acts always from an emotional, not an intellectual stimulus.*]

[*LIGHT cue # 2.*]

CLEOTA. [*From above down Right settee.*] Doctah Da-man doan talk up. He kinda muffles.

ELLEN. [*Picks up magazines on down Left table. Crossing up Left to bookcase with them.*] I'm afraid it's you that kind of muffles.

CLEOTA. Yessum. Miz Turner, Ah'm fixin' them hor doves for the pahty Did you say put dem black seed ones in de oven?

ELLEN. [*At bookcase.*] Black seed ones? Oh, heavens, Cleota, you're not heating the caviar?

CLEOTA. No'm, ah ain't heatin' it, but taste lak' sumpin' oughtta be done to it.

ELLEN. [*Crossing up Right.*] It's to be served cold. Here, you pick up the rest of the magazines. I'll take a look at the canapés. [*Exits to dining room.*]

CLEOTA. Yessum. Ah ain't no hand at 'em. People where Ah worked last jus' drank without eatin' anything. [*She comes down Right to magazines, settee down Right. Sound of whistling;* TOMMY TURNER *enters Left. He is a young associate professor, thirty-three years old. He wears glasses, is rather more charming than handsome. His clothes are a little baggy. He has a way of disarranging his hair with his hands, so that he looks like a puzzled spaniel at times. He is carrying chrysanthemums and two bottles of liquor, wrapped in paper and tied with string.*] Oh, hello, Mr. Turner!

TOMMY. [*Putting flowers and bottles on sofa.*] Hello, Cleota! [*Removes and hangs up coat and hat.*]

CLEOTA. [*Taking magazines upstage to bookcase up*

Right Center.] You bettah not mess up dis room, 'cause dey is guess comin'.

TOMMY. All right, Cleota. I'll be good.

[CLEOTA *exits to dining room up Right.* TOMMY *picks up bundles, comes Right Center—looks for place to put down bottles—puts them on chair Right Center—unwraps flowers, throwing paper on floor—throws string down Center—sticks flowers in vase in middle of other flowers; sees book, picks it up, looks at it disapprovingly, looks upstairs and makes a gesture of disgust, throws it in waste-basket—crosses to pick up liquor.*]

ELLEN. [*Enters from dining room up Right. Crossing to* TOMMY.] Hello, dear!

TOMMY. Hello, Ellen! Those are for you. [*Indicates his flowers.*]

ELLEN. Oh, thank you, Tommy. They're lovely. [*Surveys the flowers.*]

TOMMY. The ones in the middle.

ELLEN. Yes—

TOMMY. I got the liquor, too.

ELLEN. [*Taking* TOMMY'S *flowers out of vase Right.*] Did you get the right kind? [*Picks up paper.*]

TOMMY. I got both kinds.

[ELLEN *puts paper in waste-basket—crosses above* TOMMY *to Right Center—picks up string Center.*]

ELLEN. Tommy, you're a house-wrecker, but you're nice.

[*Kisses him—then crosses up Center to sofa. Puts flowers on sofa.*]

TOMMY. Did I do something right?

ELLEN. Cleota— [*Takes vase from table up Center— starts across for dining room door up Right.*] Cleota, will you fill this vase with water, please? [*Hands it to* CLEOTA *in doorway—comes to table Right behind sofa.*] What became of the book that was on this table?

TOMMY. That? Oh, I threw it in the waste-basket. It's trash.

ELLEN. [*Rescuing book.*] But you can't throw it away. Wally gave it to Patricia.

TOMMY. Oh, he did?

ELLEN. Besides, it's just the right color for this room. [VOICES *off-scene up Left.* ELLEN *crosses Left to up Center sofa—picks up flowers.*]

PAT'S VOICE. [*Off—up Left.*] Oh, Wally, quit arguing! [*Door is opened, and* PAT *backs into room.*] I'm going to dinner with Mike, and then to the rally with you. You can't feed me at the training table. [*Hangs coat up on wall hooks. She is a pretty, lively girl of 19 or 20.*]

WALLY. [*Appears in doorway. He is six-feet-one, and weighs 190 pounds, mostly muscle. He is full of energy and health, and not without a good deal of naive charm.*] Aw, that guy Barnes! I don't see why you have to— Oh, how do you do, Mrs. Turner—Professor Turner?
                              [*LIGHT cue # 3.*]

TOMMY. Hello, Butch!

ELLEN. [*Carries flowers to Center of upstage table.*] That's Wally Myers.

TOMMY. Oh, hello!

WALLY. [*Crossing into room a step.*] Oh, has Butch been coming here, too?

[TOMMY *crosses down Right.*]

PATRICIA. [*Pushing* WALLY.] Go on, get out of here, half-back. I have to get dressed. [*Crosses into room— crosses to Right Center chair.*] Hey, Ellen, excited about seeing the great Ferguson, again? He just drove up to the Beta House in a Deusenberg! [*Sits chair Right Center.*]

[CLEOTA *re-enters with vase;* ELLEN *takes it;* CLEOTA *exits.*]

ELLEN. Did you see him?

PATRICIA. No, the kids were telling me. Has he still got his hair?

ELLEN. [*Arranging flowers up Center table.*] I haven't seen him in ten years. We'll soon find out.

[TOMMY *crosses to down Right.*]

WALLY. [*Crosses to Left end up Center sofa.*] Say, is he coming here?

ELLEN. Yes. Why don't you come back and meet him, Wally? You can tell him all about the game tomorrow.

WALLY. Gee, thanks! But nobody could tell Joe Ferguson anything about a football game. He's all-time All-American, you know. [*Crosses to door up Left.*] Well, thanks, Mrs. Turner. I'll be back. See you later, Pat. [*Exits up Left.*]

PATRICIA. [*Closes door; then opens it and sticks head into room.*] So long! [*Sits chair Right Center. Takes bottle of nail-polish from her pocket book and starts to fix run in stocking.*]

TOMMY. [*From down Right.*] Does he mean that now Joe belongs to the ages, like Lincoln? [*Lights cigarette.*]

ELLEN. Um-hum, in a way.

TOMMY. [*Has picked several magazines from bookcase up Right Center and is looking through them. Crossing Left to bookcase.*] Well, I suppose he has passed into legend. I used to admire him myself—almost.

ELLEN. [*From up Center.*] Pat, why don't you and Michael stay here for dinner? Supper, rather. It's just a bite. We're all going out to eat after the rally.

PATRICIA. No, thanks. You know how Mike feels about Mr. Keller. He'd spit in his eye.

TOMMY. [*Crossing to down Left settee.*] Why do we have to have Ed Keller to this party?

ELLEN. Oh, Joe has to have someone to talk football with. Ed's his closest friend here. He practically paid Joe's way through college. You can stand the Kellers one night. [*Puts books from up Center table in up Right Center bookcase.*]

TOMMY. Just barely. I don't know how to entertain trustees. [*Sits settee Left.*]

PATRICIA. Well, you'd better be entertaining tonight

with the great Ferguson coming. [*Rises; crossing up Right to stair landing.*] Weren't you engaged to him once, Ellen?

ELLEN. Not officially. Just for fun.

PATRICIA. [*Starting up stairs.*] Baby, that can be dangerous, too! [*Exits.*]

[TOMMY *has found an article in "Harper's" and is reading.*]

ELLEN. [*Arranging flowers up Center.*] Oh, Dean Damon phoned, Tommy.

TOMMY. What'd he want?

ELLEN. I don't know. Cleota answered the phone.

TOMMY. Oh—I see— Oh, I'll bet I know. I saw the Dean this morning. What do you think?

ELLEN. Oh, I don't know— Oh, Tommy, you don't mean—?

TOMMY. Yes, I do.

ELLEN. [*Crossing down Left to* TOMMY *and kissing his forehead.*] Oh Tommy, that's wonderful! It's three hundred and fifty more a year, isn't it?

TOMMY. Five hundred! I'm no piker.

ELLEN. Well, you certainly deserve it.

TOMMY. Now I can get you that fur coat next February People must think I let you freeze in the winter.

ELLEN. [*Crossing up Center to table.*] No, they don't. And, don't worry about me— [*At flowers.*] You need some new things, yourself.—I love the flowers, Tommy. And this promotion couldn't have come on a better day for me. Do you know what day it is? [*Crossing Right.*]

[*LIGHTS. Floor cans out. Start stay X-ray down.*]

TOMMY. Friday, isn't it? Why?

ELLEN. Oh, nothing—never mind. [*Down Right. Glances around room. Throws string from flowers in waste-basket.*] What became of all the match-boxes? [*Crossing Left to* TOMMY.] I had one in each ash tray.

TOMMY. [*She is digging in his pockets.*] I haven't seen any match-boxes. [*She finds two. He smiles guiltily.*] Say, you look very pretty tonight. That's a new dress, isn't it?

ELLEN. [*Right of Left settee.*] No— It's my hair that's bothering you. It's done a new way—

TOMMY. Doesn't bother me. I like it.

ELLEN. [*Looking around.*] One more.

TOMMY. Oh, you exaggerate this match-box thing. Oh! [*Hands her one.* ELLEN *crosses and puts it on table up Center.*] I ought to take you out to dinner more and show you off.

ELLEN. [*Up Center table.*] Well, we're going out tonight after the rally.

TOMMY. I mean just the two of us. Tonight will be just like old times. Remember how Joe was always horning in on our dinner dates? I don't believe we ever had one that he didn't come over and diagram the Washington Monument play or something on the tablecloth with a pencil.

ELLEN. [*Crossing Right to Right end of table.*] Statue of Liberty play, darling.

TOMMY. He was always coming. I never saw him going.

ELLEN. There's still one missing. [*Crossing Left to* TOMMY.]

TOMMY. I haven't got it— [*Finds match-box.*] I'll bet Joe does something to get his wife down. Probably cleans his guns with doilies. [ELLEN *crossing Right puts box on down Right table.*] Clumsy guy. Always knocking knives and forks on the floor.

ELLEN. He wasn't clumsy. He was very graceful. [*Crossing to up Right Center bookcase, fixes books.*] He was a swell dancer.

TOMMY. I remember he got the first and the last dance with you, the last time we all went to a dance together.

ELLEN. Phi Psi Christmas dance, wasn't it?

TOMMY. No, the May Dance. Out at the Trowbridge Farm. Remember how it rained?

ELLEN. [*Crosses down to Right table.*] I remember I had the last dance with Joe because you disappeared somewhere.

TOMMY. No, I was watching—from behind some ferns.

ELLEN. [*Fixes flowers.*] They played "Three O'Clock in the Morning" and "Who"? It was a lovely night, wasn't it?

TOMMY. No, it poured down. [*Rises; crossing up Left to bookcase.*] You and Joe were dancing out on the terrace when it started. You both got soaked, but you kept right on dancing.

ELLEN. [*Down Left to coffee table—straightens it. Picks up magazine.*] Oh, yes, I remember. My dress was ruined.

TOMMY. [*Crossing to Left Center.*] You were shining wet—like Venus and Triton.

ELLEN. Why didn't you cut in? [*Crossing up Left to bookcase with magazines from down Left table; puts them in bookcase.*]

TOMMY. I had a cold. Besides, my feet hurt. [*Crossing to up Right platform.*] I'll dress. [*DOORBELL rings.*] I hope he isn't here already.

[ELLEN *admits* DAMON *and* MICHAEL. DAMON, *the head of the English Department, is a tall, thin, distinguished-looking man of some 65 years. He has gray hair, eyes capable of twinkling through glasses whose rims he has a habit of peering over. He talks slowly, selecting his words, in a voice at once compelling and humorous. He often hesitates, peers over his glasses before saying the last word of a phrase or a sentence.* MICHAEL BARNES *is a Senior in the Arts College, an intensely serious young man and a fine literary student. The older people who surround him find his youthful grimness about life's problems sometimes amusing, but more frequently alarming.*]

ELLEN. Oh, come in, Doctor Damon.

MICHAEL. How do you do, sir? [*Crosses down Left to radio cabinet.*]

DAMON. [*Crossing to* TOMMY.] Hello, Thomas!

ELLEN. [*Crossing door.*] Where's Mrs. Damon?

DAMON. [*Crossing down to Center.*] I shall pick her up and bring her along shortly for the festivities. This is in the nature of an unofficial call.

TOMMY. [*Crossing down Left to* MICHAEL.] Hello, Michael! You both look a little grim. Has anything happened?

DAMON. [*Showing paper.*] Michael has written another of his fiery editorials.

PATRICIA. [*Runs down the stairs.*] Ellen, did you see my—oh! How do you do, Doctor Damon? Hi, Michael!

MICHAEL. H'lo! [*Crosses upstage.*]

DAMON. Sit down, my dear. [PATRICIA *sits Left end of settee Right.* MICHAEL *crosses down Left.*] I have here an editorial written by Michael for *The Lit,* which comes out tomorrow. Perhaps, to save time, one of us should read it aloud-- [*Reading.*] "When this so-called University forces such men out of its faculty as Professor Kennedy, [ELLEN *sits down Left.* TOMMY *crosses to up Left Center.*] Professor Sykes, and Professor Chapman, because they have been ignorantly called Reds, it surrenders its right to be called a seat of learning. It admits that it is nothing more nor less than a training school—you will recognize the voice of our good friend, Hutchins, of Chicago—a training school for bond salesmen, farmers, real-estate dealers, and ambulance chasers. It announces to the world that its faculty is subservient—" [DAMON *peers over glasses at* MICHAEL.]

MICHAEL. [*Is pacing up and down Left. Crossing Right to* DAMON.] Oh, I didn't mean you, of course, Doctor Damon.

DAMON. "—that its faculty is subservient to its trustees, and that its trustees represent a political viewpoint which must finally emerge under its proper name, which is— Fascism."

[TOMMY *sits up Center sofa.*]

PATRICIA. [*From down Right. Rising.*] Oh, Michael! There you go again!

DAMON. [*A step to her.*] Wait till you hear where he has actually gone.

[MICHAEL *crosses to bookcase up Right Center.*]

PATRICIA. Isn't that all?

DAMON. Unhappily, there is more.

[TOMMY *lights cigarette.*]

PATRICIA. [*Sits.*] Oh, Lord!

DAMON. [*Crosses Center.*] "These professors were not Reds. They were distinguished liberals. Let us thank God that we still have one man left who is going ahead teaching what he believes should be taught."

TOMMY. [*Lights cigarette.*] Who's that?

[MICHAEL *crosses down.*]

DAMON. "He is not afraid to bring up even the Sacco-Vanzetti case. He has read to his classes on the same day Vanzetti's last statement and Lincoln's letter to Mrs. Bixby." I hope we are not alienating the many friends of Abraham Lincoln. "The hounds of bigotry and [TOMMY *rises, crosses Right to* DAMON. MICHAEL *crosses up.*] reaction will, of course, be set upon the trail of this courageous teacher, but, if they think they are merely on the spoor of a lamb they are destined to the same disappointment as the hunters who in chasing the wild boar, came accidentally upon a tigress and her cubs. [ELLEN *looks at* MICHAEL.] Our hats are off to Professor Thomas Turner of the English Department." That's all.

ELLEN. Tommy?

TOMMY. Michael, I think you might have consulted me. about this. [*Crosses to* MICHAEL *at up Left Center.*]

PATRICIA. [*Rises.*] Michael, you fool! They'll kick you out of school for this—and Tommy too!

ELLEN. You never told me you had brought up the Sacco-Vanzetti case in your classes, Tommy.

DAMON. [*Crossing to* TOMMY.] Yes, just what is this Vanzetti letter you have read?

TOMMY. I haven't read it yet.

MICHAEL. When you told me the other day you were going to read it, I thought you meant that day.

TOMMY. No, Michael. I just meant some day. But I was talking to you as a friend, I was not giving an interview to an editor.

ELLEN. But why were you going to read this letter, Tommy?

[MICHAEL *crosses Left to bookcase; then down Left.*]

TOMMY. Because it's a fine piece of English composition, and I'm teaching a class in English composition. An obscure little class. I don't want any publicity, Michael. I just want to be left alone.

ELLEN. But nobody thinks of Vanzetti as a writer, Tommy.

TOMMY. It happens that he developed into an extraordinary writer. [*Crossing to* DAMON.] I don't think you could help being interested in the letter yourself, Doctor Damon.

DAMON. You would be surprised at my strength of will in these matters, Thomas. What I am interested in is preserving some air of academic calm here at Midwestern—

PATRICIA. [*Crossing to Right Center.*] You don't want to get Tommy kicked out of school, do you, Michael?

MICHAEL. No. I didn't think of that. [*Crossing to Left Center.*] I thought Mr. Turner was about the only man we had left who would read whatever he wanted to to his classes. [*Up to* TOMMY.] I thought he was the one man who would stand up to these stadium builders.

[DAMON *crosses to up Center.*]

TOMMY. [*At Left Center.*] I'm not standing up to anyone, Michael. I'm not challenging anyone. This is just an innocent little piece I wanted to read.

[MICHAEL *crosses up Left to bookcase, then downstage.*]

ELLEN. [*Rises. Crossing to* TOMMY.] I'm sure this piece must be fine, Tommy, but you can't read it now. Keller and the other trustees kicked Don Chapman out last month for doing things just as harmless as this. [*Turn-*

ing to MICHAEL.] You'll have to change that editorial, Michael.

[TOMMY *crosses Right.*]

MICHAEL. I can't. The magazines were run off the presses last night. They've already been delivered to the news stands.

DAMON. They go on sale in the morning. [*Crossing Left to* ELLEN.] I think that our—er—tigress here may have to issue a denial tomorrow. After all, he hasn't read it yet.

ELLEN. [*Crossing to* TOMMY.] Yes, and you mustn't read it now.

PATRICIA. [*Crossing Left to* DAMON.] Will Michael be kicked out of school, Doctor Damon?

[TOMMY *sits Right settee.*]

DAMON. Sufficient unto the day is the evil thereof, my dear. [*Crosses up. Gets hat.*]

PATRICIA. [*Crossing down Left to* MICHAEL.] There! You see—

DAMON. [*Crossing down to* TOMMY.] Of course I quite understand how you meant to present this letter, Thomas; but our good friend Mr. Keller would not. [TOMMY *starts to speak.* DAMON *stops him.*] Do not underestimate Mr. Edward K. Keller. He rolls like the juggernaut over the careers of young professors.

TOMMY. I know.

DAMON. [*Crossing up Left to door.*] Since he must be

with us tonight let us confine our conversation to the
—woeful inadequacies of the Illinois team.

TOMMY. [*Rising.*] It isn't Illinois we're playing—it's
Michigan.

[*LIGHT cue # 4. Sneak balconies up.*]

DAMON. Oh, I must remember that. [*Exits up Left.*]

PATRICIA. [*Down Left.*] There, you see! You will be
kicked out.

MICHAEL. He didn't say that.

PATRICIA. Yes, he did. You needn't bother to come back
for me, Michael. [*Crossing towards stairs.*] I'm staying
here for supper. [*Runs up stairs.*]

MICHAEL. [*Crossing to Left Center.*] I see. I'm sorry,
Mr. Turner. I guess I got—well—carried away.

TOMMY. [*Crossing Left to* MICHAEL.] I know, Michael.
Sometimes, when I see that light in your eye I wish I
could be carried away too.

MICHAEL. Yes sir. [*Exits up Left. Slight pause.*]

TOMMY. [*Crossing up Left a few steps after him.*]
Well—

ELLEN. [*Crossing to* TOMMY *Left Center.*] I'm sorry,
Tommy.

TOMMY. Oh it's all right. Maybe I can read this thing
later on, after all the fuss quiets down—say next spring.

ELLEN. It would still be dangerous.

TOMMY. [*Crossing up Right.*] Yes, I guess it would.
[*Turns back to* ELLEN.] I know I'm not a tiger, but I
don't like to be thought of as a pussy-cat either.

ELLEN. It's getting late. [*Crossing Right to* TOMMY.] You'd better go and put on that gray suit I laid out for you. [*Crossing Left Center.*] And be sure your socks are right side out, and Tommy—don't try to be a tiger in front of Ed Keller.

TOMMY. [*At stair landing.*] I won't. I'm scared of those Neanderthal men. I'll talk about football.

ELLEN. Thank you, darling. [*Crossing Left to mantel.*] That's swell. You know how Joe is—always cheerful. And we do want it to be a good party. [*Straightens mantel.*]

TOMMY. I'll be cheerful. I'll be merry and bright. I'll be the most cheerful son-of-a-gun in this part of the country. [*He sings as he exits up the stairs.*]
      "Who's afraid of the Big Bad Wolf?
      The Big Bad Wolf?
      The Big Bad Wolf?
      Who's afraid tum-tee-ump—"

[ELLEN *looks after him doubtfully. DOORBELL rings.*]

ELLEN. [*Calling upstairs.*] Hurry, Tommy! They're here! [*Crosses to Left door; admits* JOE FERGUSON, *followed by* WALLY MYERS.] Hello, Joe!

JOE. Ellen, darling! How are you? Gosh, you look great! Why, you're younger and prettier than ever! If I were a braver man, I'd kiss you. Doggone it, I *will* kiss you! [*Kisses her on cheek, hugs her, lifts her off the floor— whirls her down to Center.* JOE *is big, handsome, successful, and pleasing, about 35.*]

[WALLY *closes door—stands up Left Center.*]

ELLEN. It's terribly nice to see you again, Joe. If I were a younger woman, I'd say it's been all of ten years.

JOE. [*Crossing up to sofa; puts box of flowers down.*] Gosh, this is swell! Where's the great Thomas?

ELLEN. Tommy will be right down. I see Wally found you—so you've met?

[JOE *crosses to* WALLY, *who helps him take off coat and hangs it on hook.*]

JOE. Yeh. We joined forces outside. [*Thanks* WALLY.]

ELLEN. Come on over here and sit down. [*Crossing to down Left settee and sitting Left end.*]

JOE. I forgot to ask you Wally, who's going in at the other half tomorrow? Stalenkiwiecz?

WALLY. No, sir. Wierasocka.

JOE. Oh, is he?

WALLY. Yeh. He's a Beta. From Oregon.

JOE. Oh, yeh—yeh, I know him.

WALLY. [*Crossing and sitting Center down Left settee.*] Stalenkiwiecz is laid up. They think he's got whooping cough.

JOE. That's bad! [*Crossing down Left.—To* ELLEN. *Looking for room on settee.*] I've got a thousand fish on that game. [*Sits Right end settee. It is very crowded.*]

WALLY. I think it's safe, all right, Mr. Ferguson, but I wish we had you. Stalenkiwiecz, Wierasocka, Myers and Whirling Joe Ferguson.

ELLEN. Do they still call you that, Joe?

JOE. Oh, sure, remember how—

WALLY. Say, he was the greatest open-field runner there ever was.

ELLEN. Yes, Joe. How does it happen you've never even—

WALLY. Why, you made Red Grange look like a cripple.

JOE. Aw, they say you're not so bad yourself. Say Ellen, how's—

WALLY. Aw, I'm just fair, that's all. [*Produces a clipping from coat pocket.*] This is what Grantland Rice said about me. [*Hands it to* JOE.]

JOE. Yeh.—Too bad this is Wally's last year. We're going to miss him—eh, Ellen?

ELLEN. Have you got anything to do, Wally?

WALLY. Well—the Coach wants me to help him with the back-field next season. Not much money in it, of course.

JOE. [*Hands clipping back to* WALLY.] Well, if you want my advice, don't go in for coaching. I had a sweet offer from Cincinnati in 'Twenty-nine. Remember that, Ellen?

ELLEN. I remember very well. Do you remember when—

WALLY. Nineteen twenty-nine! [*Leaning forward meditatively.*]—I was only twelve years old then—

TOMMY. [*Comes downstairs. Crossing to* JOE.] Hello, Joe! It's nice to see you again!

JOE. [*Rises. Crossing to him.* WALLY *rises.*] Tommy, old man, how are you? Ten years! Teaching must be

good for you. And Ellen, here, looks like a million
bucks! That reminds me—I came laden with gifts.
[*Turns and almost runs into* WALLY. *He goes and gets
flowers up Center sofa.*] These are a few flowering
weeds— [*Crosses to* ELLEN.]

[WALLY *still behind* JOE.]

ELLEN. [*From Left settee.*] Thank you, Joe. They're
lovely. Tommy, will you call Cleota?

[WALLY *leans over back of settee Left.*]

TOMMY. Sure! [*Goes into dining room, calls.*] Cleota!

ELLEN. It's fun to get flowers. Very festive.

JOE. Oh, it's nothing much, but I wanted you to know
I remembered the great day. Think I'd forget it was
your birthday?

ELLEN. You never used to. [TOMMY *re-enters.* ELLEN
crosses to Center and meets TOMMY.] Tommy gave me
some flowering weeds, too—for my birthday.

TOMMY. For your—oh—yes— Not such nice ones, I'm
afraid. [*To* ELLEN.] I'm a lucky man. [*Turns back. She
pats his hand.*]

[CLEOTA *enters to* ELLEN *from dining room.*]

ELLEN. Will you find something to put these in, Cleota?

CLEOTA. [*Sighs.*] Yassum. Ah guess Ah'll hafta put 'em
in de sink wit dat ice. [*Exits to dining room.*]

JOE. Boy, it's sure great to be here! [*Crossing down
Left.*]

[WALLY *crosses around down Left to fireplace bench.*]

TOMMY. It's nice to have you.—Staying long?

JOE. Got to be in Washington next week. [*Noticing bookcases.*] Well, Tommy, I see you've still got a lot of books.

TOMMY. Oh, yes.

JOE. You know I never get a chance to read books. [*Sits Left settee.*]

WALLY. Say, you must have a swell job! [*Sits on bench front of fireplace.*]

[ELLEN *crosses to Left Center.*]

JOE. By the time I get through at night, I'm lucky if I can keep up with what's going on in the world. Way things are changing, you gotta do that. I take fifteen magazines. That keeps me busy.

ELLEN [*Crosses Left to* TOMMY. *Takes his arm.*] Tommy's had several articles in *Harper's* and the *Atlantic*.

JOE. No! Say, that's fine! But you'll have to boil them down to *The Reader's Digest* to reach me, Tommy. [JOE *and* WALLY *laugh.*] You know, that's a great little magazine.

TOMMY. Do you like buillon cubes?

ELLEN. [*Hurrying him out.*] Tommy, you'd better make a drink.

TOMMY. [*Crossing below her to up Right door.*] Yes. We have a lot of celebrating to do. [*Crosses into dining room calling* "Cleota."]

ELLEN. How've you been, Joe? [*Sits next to* JOE.]

JOE. Fine, except for a little sinus trouble.

WALLY. You know, Mrs. Turner, I recognized him right away from that big picture in the gym.

[TOMMY *re-enters with bowl of ice. Crosses to up Right table; mixes drinks.*]

ELLEN. That's fine. How's Brenda? I meant to ask before.

JOE. Fine! Great! Little heavier, maybe. We're being divorced, you know.

ELLEN. But I didn't know. Oh, Joe, I'm sorry.

JOE. Nothing to be sorry about. It's just one of those things.

[JOE *and* WALLY *laugh.*]

TOMMY. [*From up Right.*] What's the matter?

ELLEN. Joe and his wife are breaking up.

TOMMY. Oh, that's too bad.

JOE. No, it's all fine. We're both taking it in our stride. Took her out to dinner last week—along with her new boy friend.

[WALLY *takes this big—very funny.*]

TOMMY. Wasn't that rather complicated?

ELLEN. Oh, you're not up to date, Tommy. That's the modern way of doing things.

JOE. Sure! Take it in your stride. Gosh, Ellen, I can't take my eyes off you. [*This is cute so* WALLY *laughs again.* JOE *notices* TOMMY *watching.*] Nice little place you got here. [*Rises.*] Need any help, Tommy? I'm a demon on Manhattans. [*Crosses above Left settee to* TOMMY *up Right.*]

[*DOORBELL rings.*]

TOMMY. I'm all right, thanks.

JOE. [*Crossing down Right.*] I hope that's Ed, the old scoundrel.

ELLEN. [*Goes to the door Left and admits the* DAMONS.] I'm so glad— Hello, Mrs. Damon!

BLANCHE. [*Entering.*] Hello, Ellen dear! How do you do, Mr. Turner?

[WALLY *rises.*]

ELLEN. [*Coming down with* BLANCHE.] You must know Joe Ferguson.

BLANCHE. Oh, of course!

ELLEN. This is Mrs. Damon, Joe. You remember Dean Damon?

JOE. Yes indeed! Nice to see you again, sir.

DAMON. [*Crossing to him and shaking hands.*] Back for the slaughter of the—uh—Michigan innocents, eh?

JOE. That's right.

[ELLEN *and* BLANCHE *have crossed down Left to* WALLY. DAMON *crosses up; puts coat on up Left chair; hat on up Center table.*]

ELLEN. Mrs. Damon, may I present Mr. Myers?

BLANCHE. Oh, yes of course we all know about our great fullback.

[TOMMY *gives away cocktails.* JOE *gets cocktail from* TOMMY.]

WALLY. How do you do?

ELLEN. Let me help you with your coat.

BLANCHE. Thank you, dear. [*To* WALLY.] Tell me, are you nervous about the game?

WALLY. No, ma'am.

BLANCHE. Not the least little bit?

[ELLEN *takes* BLANCHE'S *coat up to window seat; stands* DAMON'S *umbrella above sofa.*]

WALLY. No, ma'am.

BLANCHE. That's nice. [*Sits down Left.*]

DAMON. [*Crossing Right to* JOE.] I remember you not only from the gridiron but from my Shakespeare class. You slept very quietly.

JOE. You know, I never did finish reading *Hamlet*. I always wondered how that came out. [*He laughs heartily.*]

[DAMON *laughs politely.*]

TOMMY. [*Crossing Left with two cocktails.*] Does anybody mind a Manhattan?

BLANCHE. Oh, Ellen! Could we have sherry?

ELLEN. Certainly. Tommy—

TOMMY. Sherry coming right up. [*Crossing down Left to* WALLY.] Here, Wally. [*Gives him cocktail.*]

WALLY. No, thanks. I'm in training.

TOMMY. [*Crossing to* DAMON.] Well, just hold it. [WALLY *puts glass down on down Left table.*] Sherry for you too, Doctor Damon?

DAMON. When Mrs. Damon says we, she means me. Sherry, thanks.

[TOMMY *crosses up Right.* DAMON *crosses down Left to* BLANCHE, *then up to bookcase Left.*]

BLANCHE. [*Drinking other cocktail.*] A little sherry is such fun. [WALLY *offers her cigarette from box on coffee table.*] No thanks, I'll smoke my "Spuds"! [*She does.*]

[WALLY *lights* BLANCHE's *cigarette.*]

PATRICIA. [*Coming downstairs.*] Hello, everybody!

[*General* "hellos!"]

ELLEN. [*Brings her down to* JOE.] This is my sister Patricia.

PATRICIA. How do you do?

JOE. [*Admiring her.*] How do you *do?* My goodness! Why, you're as big and pretty as your sister. How about a drink?

PATRICIA. No, thanks. [*To* ELLEN, *crosses Center.*] Still has his hair. [TOMMY *looks up at this.* PATRICIA, *crossing to* WALLY.] Hello, Wally!

[TOMMY *pours sherry for* DAMONS.]

WALLY. Hi, Pat! Look, can I pick you up at Hennick's a little earlier?

PATRICIA. I'm not going to Hennick's. I'm eating here. That date's off.

WALLY. [*Crossing to* PATRICIA.] With Barnes? Say, that's swell. [*Smacks* PATRICIA *on the back, almost knocking her down. Crosses to* ELLEN.] I got to run along, Mrs. Turner. Nice party. [*Shakes* ELLEN's *hand heartily. Crosses to* JOE.] Glad I met you, Joe—I mean, Mr. Ferguson. [*They shake hands.*] I'll be seeing you. Goodbye, everybody! I'll go out the back way. [*Exits down Right.*]

JOE. Take it easy, old man. Don't break a leg on me. Remember, I've got a thousand fish on that game. [*Follows* WALLY *out.*]

WALLY. [*Off.*] I won't.

BLANCHE. He's a handsome boy, Patricia. [*DOOR-BELL rings.*] And seems very healthy.

PATRICIA. I have to keep in training for him. [*Crosses to fireplace. Sits down stage end of bench.*]

[TOMMY *crosses up Left to door.* DAMON *sits upper end fireplace bench.*]

TOMMY. I'll get it.

[*The* KELLERS *come into the room.* ED KELLER *is a big, loud, slightly bald man of about thirty-eight, heavy around the middle. He is a prosperous real-estate man, owns the Keller Building, is a trustee and as such, the biggest voice and strongest hand on the Board.* MYRTLE KELLER, *also in her late thirties, dresses well and is not bad-looking, was once pretty, but is now a slightly faded blonde.*]

ED. Hello, Ellen! Hi, Turner! Where is he? [*Passes* TOMMY *fast, without handshake:* JOE *reappears;* ED *comes down and meets* JOE *Right Center. This is a typical meeting between two old friends of the hale-and-hearty, back-slapping variety who haven't met for years.*] Hiya, you old rascal! Hahya, boy?

JOE. [*Running to meet him, so that they clinch in the middle of the room, hugging, slapping backs, etc.* ELLEN *is helping* MYRTLE *take off her coat up Left.*] Hello, you old son-of-a-gun! How are you, Ed? [*Crosses to* MYRTLE.] Hello, Myrtle! Gosh, I'm glad to see you! [*Hugs her.*]

MYRTLE. [*Screams.*] I'm glad to see you, too! Ellen—

JOE. [*Back to* ED.] Gee, you're looking swell, Ed, old boy, old boy!

ED. Judas Priest, this is swell! How are you anyway, Joe? [*Resumes back-slapping.*]

[*The* MEN'S *voices predominate during the following.*]

JOE. Fine! Swell! Never better. You've put on a little weight, eh, Eddie? And what's happened to the crowning glory?

ED. Worry: real-estate, Roosevelt. Wonder I got any left.

[ED *takes off coat and hat.* TOMMY *puts them on window seat.*]

MYRTLE. How do you do, Doctor Damon? How do you do, Mrs. Damon? Haven't seen you in a long, long time. Hello, Patricia — Oh, quiet down! Ed! [*Sits down Left.*] Are we late, Ellen?

ELLEN. Not at all. Just in time for the canapés. [*Puts* MYRTLE'S *coat up Left chair.*]

JOE. How long's it been, Ed? Seven, eight years, isn't it?

ED. Eight, anyway.

[TOMMY *crosses down Right.*]

ELLEN. [*Crosses to* ED.] Look, you two, will you break it up and say hello to people?

ED. All right, Ellen, but it sure is fine to see The Whirler again. [*Crossing Left to* DAMON.] How do you do, Doctor Damon? Not drinking straight Scotch, I hope?

[JOE *moves down Right.* ELLEN *goes up Right for drinks.*]

DAMON. [*Rising.*] If I did that, my stomach—and Mrs. Damon—would punish me severely.

ELLEN. [*Crossing Left to* ED.] Won't you have a cocktail, Ed? [*Crosses to* ED *with drink.*]

ED. [*Moves to up Right Center.*] Thanks.

JOE. [*Down Right.*] Say, this is Ellen's birthday. How about a little toast?

[DAMON *crosses to Left bookcase.*]

TOMMY. Well, fill 'em up. [*Pours drinks, one for him·self. Sits down Right.*]

ED. [*Crossing Center.*] Well, happy birthday, Ellen!

[*They drink;* ED *starts the "Happy Birthday To You" song, and they* ALL *sing. It is obvious* TOMMY *is bored; he takes a drink—then noticing everybody standing, he rises, sings the last line very off key.* CLEOTA *enters up*

Right, comes up behind DAMON *up Left with plate of canapés.*]

CLEOTA. [*After song dies.*] Hor doves?

DAMON. I beg your pardon—oh! Thank you. [*Takes one.*]

JOE. [*As* TOMMY *pours another round.*] Let's drink one toast to The Big Red Team. What do you say?

[TOMMY *starts humming "The Big Bad Wolf."* CLEOTA *is passing canapés to* LADIES *on settee down Left.*]

ED. The Big Red Team.

[MYRTLE *gets deep in conversation with* BLANCHE.]

TOMMY. [*Singing softly; crossing around Right above* JOE *and* ED *to Center.*]
"The Big Red Team—
Big Red Team.
Who's afraid of The Big Red Team—"

ED. What's that?

TOMMY. Huh? [ED *glares at him. To* ELLEN.] What did I do?

[ED *crosses to* JOE *at down Right settee.*]

ELLEN. [*Meets him Center.*] Tommy! You'd better eat something. Those cocktails are strong.

TOMMY. [*Crossing Right to* JOE.] I'm doing all right, honey. [ED *sits Left end down Right settee.*] How's everything in Detroit, Joe?

JOE. [*Taking a canapé* ELLEN *is serving.*] I don't know. all right, I guess. [*Sits Right end down Right settee.*]

ELLEN. Tommy means Pittsburgh. The Bryson Steel Company is in Pittsburgh, Tommy. [*Crosses to* CLEOTA *up Center.*]

[CLEOTA *gives* ELLEN *tray and exits dining room.*]

TOMMY. [*Stands back of chair Right Center.*] Oh, yes, sure. Well, how's everything in Pittsburgh?

[DAMON *sits fireplace bench.*]

JOE. Well, it might be worse.

ED. [*Stuffing caviar into his mouth.*] Couldn't be much worse out here.

TOMMY. Have a drink.

ELLEN. [*Crossing down Left to* MYRTLE—*serving canapés.*] How are the kids, Myrtle?

MYRTLE. They're all right. The baby has some kind of rash on her little hips, but it's nothing, really. Makes her cross, though.

ED. [*To* JOE.] Time sure does fly. Now Buster wants to go to Princeton. No matter how you watch 'em, they get in with the wrong kids.

[TOMMY *crosses up Left.*]

[*The* WOMEN'S *voices predominate.* ELLEN *serves canapés down Left.*]

BLANCHE. How's your sister?

MYRTLE. They took a stone out of her as big as a wal-

JOE. [*Spreading this.*] I remember when I actually got along with only one car, and thought it was plenty. Now I've got three,

nut. She can't weigh more than ninety pounds.

and the bills are terrific— Do you know what my gas bill was last month?

[DAMON *rises, bored and crosses up Left to bookcase— picks out book and glances through it.*]

BLANCHE. They cut old Mrs. Wilmot open for the same trouble, and didn't find a thing!

[*Ad lib from* MEN *down Right.*]

MYRTLE. [*Turns to* ED *who is talking to* JOE *down Right.*] Ed, when was it I had that impacted tooth out?

ED. [*Hastily stopping conversation with* JOE.] Seven years ago. Year the banks closed. 'Thirty-three. [*Right back to* JOE.]

TOMMY. [*Center.*] Fill 'em up. [*Pours himself another.*]

ELLEN. [*Crossing Right to* TOMMY.] Tommy! [*She takes shaker away from him. Returns to* LADIES.] Dividend for the women folks. Give me your glass, Myrtle. [*Crosses to* MYRTLE *down Left.*]

MYRTLE. [*Offers her glass.*] Thanks.

BLANCHE. No more for us. Mercy, we'll be light-headed.

TOMMY. [*Follows* ELLEN *over, takes shaker, pours himself another.*] But we're celebrating the homecoming game. Banks closing and everything.

JOE. How's building out here now, Ed?

TOMMY. [*Crossing Right to* ED.] Yeh, how's building?

ED. Lousy. Whatta ya expect with that man in the White House? You know what *I* think? I think he's crazy.

JOE. You know what I heard?

[*The* WOMEN *stop their talk to listen, but* JOE *whispers in* ED'S *ear.* TOMMY *crosses up Right Center, puts shaker on bookcase.*]

ED. I wouldn't be a damn bit surprised.

[ED'S *voice predominates in the following.*]

ED. Only hope for business I see is some big new industry. And he'll probably do something to ruin that.

BLANCHE. [*Sotto voce.*] Patricia, may I see the little girl's room?

MYRTLE. Me, too.

PATRICIA. Yes, I'll show you.

[*They start toward stairs.*]

MYRTLE. [*As they start upstairs.*] Is it serious?

BLANCHE. [*Disappearing upstairs.*] They took a pint of pus out of her!

[DAMON *slams book shut and looks after them: crosses down.* TOMMY *and* ELLEN *cross up Center to sofa and sit.*]

ED. Well, Doctor Damon, we men on the Board of Trustees are certainly glad that this Red scare is over.

DAMON. [*Crosses toward Center with book under his arm.*] No doubt you are.

ED. Now maybe the new stadium project will get somewhere.

DAMON. [*Crossing to down Left Center.*] And the Endowment Fund?

ED. Yeh, sure—that's important too. I'm working to convince the substantial alumni that we've got all this Parlor Pink business over and done with. Got 'em all weeded out.

[DAMON *crosses up to* ELLEN.]

JOE. Yeah—all that newspaper stuff was pretty bad.

ED. Sure! Nobody felt like coming through for anything when they read about men like Kennedy and Sykes and Chapman being in the faculty. That Chapman was nothing but a damn Red.

TOMMY. No, he wasn't, Mr. Keller. Don Chapman was a humanist.

ELLEN. We knew him very well.

JOE. How do you know he wasn't a Red, Tommy?

ED. He went to Soviet Russia for his vacation once, didn't he?

TOMMY. [*Crossing down Right to* ED.] He just went to see the Drama Festival.

ED. [*Suspiciously.*] Well, it's a mighty long way to go to see a show.

CLEOTA. [*Who has just entered up Right.*] Suppah is se'ved. [*Exits.*]

ELLEN. [*Quickly.*] Shall·we go into the dining room? It's only a salad. We're going out to eat afterwards. Come along, Ed, we don't want to miss that rally. [*She links her arm through* ED'S *and they exit up Right.*]

ED. [*Off.*] Say, that's right. I haven't missed a Michigan rally in seventeen years.

ELLEN. [*Re-enters; goes to stairs; calls up.*] Supper's ready!

[PATRICIA, BLANCHE, *and* MYRTLE *come downstairs.*]

BLANCHE. Come, Frederick. [*Takes* DAMON'S *arm and follows into dining room.*]

ELLEN. Patricia, you get a plate for Mr. Ferguson. He's the guest of honor you know.

JOE. And I'll get a plate for you, Ellen. Come on. [JOE *and* PATRICIA *exit up Right.*]

MYRTLE. [*As she goes into dining room.*] Oh, what a lovely table, Ellen!

[*During the following scene until* ED'S *re-entrance, there is the general CONVERSATION in the dining room, as* EVERYBODY *is finding his supper and beginning to eat.*]

ELLEN. [*Crossing to* TOMMY *Center.*] Tommy, don't say any more about Don Chapman tonight, please.

TOMMY. All right, I won't. Let's get something to eat. [ELLEN *takes his arm. They start for dining room.*] Joe looks better, doesn't he?

ELLEN. Better?

TOMMY. Well, bigger anyway.

[*They exit.*]

[CLEOTA *has entered with cleanup tray. She clears drinks*

and tray on down Right table; crosses to down Left table, puts dirty glasses on her tray. She is singing "I Can't Give You Anything But Love" during all this. She finds one glass with some liquor in it. After a long scrutiny she raises it to her lips, is just about to drink when she hears.]

ED. [*Off.*] Come on, Myrtle! Hurry up! Joe's got to speak at this rally.

[CLEOTA *drinks and quickly puts glass on tray and resumes song as* ED *enters and sits down Right settee.* BLANCHE *and* MYRTLE *enter with* DAMON *following them and carrying two plates.*]

BLANCHE. Frederick, put it down there on the table. [*Gestures down Left table.*]

MYRTLE. [*As they're crossing down Left.*] What makes you think there was something suspicious about it?

BLANCHE. [*Sitting down Left on Right end settee.*] Well, his family won't allow a post mortem. [DAMON *puts her plate on table, crosses up to Left bookcase with his own plate.* MYRTLE *sits Left end of down Left settee.*] Thank you, Frederick, that's fine.

[CLEOTA *has gone out.* ELLEN *enters with* JOE *to Center.* JOE *sits sofa up Center.*]

ELLEN. I hope you can all find a place to sit.

JOE. What's the matter with this? Come on, Ellen.

ELLEN. [*Smiles and sits beside him, speaking to* PATRICIA, *who appears in dining room door.*] Pat, is Tommy getting some food?

PATRICIA. Yeh, he's all right. [*Crosses down and sits on fireplace bench.*]

TOMMY. [*Entering up Right.*] Sure, I'm fine. [*Crosses Center, looking around for a place to settle.*]

ELLEN. Bring in the coffee, please, Cleota.

ED. [*Making room on the settee.*] There's room here for somebody.

TOMMY. I'll sit— [*Looks around for a place away from* ED—*only vacant space is Right Center chair.*] here.

MYRTLE. Eat your vegetables, Ed.

ED. Aw, this is a party. [*Eating like a horse from his heaped plate.*]

BLANCHE. Where's Michael Barnes this evening, Patricia? Frederick tells me he's written a remarkable editorial. [DAMON *drops his fork on plate.*] Be careful, Frederick!

ED. [*His mouth is full.*] Barnes—Barnes—? I haven't read a decent editorial since Brisbane died.

PATRICIA. Michael couldn't come. He doesn't like Mr. —er—

[ELLEN *gives* PATRICIA *a "shush" signal.*]

MYRTLE. Doesn't like what?

PATRICIA. Doesn't like parties.

BLANCHE. I'm always so interested in the *Literary Magazine*. What was the editorial, Patricia?

DAMON. [*Coming around to her Right upstage of set-*

tee.] Eat your dinner, my dear. Remember, Mr. Keller
—wants to get to the rally.

ED. Huh?

BLANCHE. What's the matter with you? [*To* PATRICIA.]
I hope I haven't said anything, dear.

[PATRICIA *shakes her head.* DAMON *moves back to book-case.*]

ED. What's going on over there? Who is this Barnes?

TOMMY. One of Patricia's beaux.

ED. Some writer!

TOMMY. He's a student. Editor on *The Literary Maga-zine.*

ED. Oh, yeah, I've heard of him. What's he done now?

ELLEN. Oh, it's nothing really.

TOMMY. Well, since it's come up, Ellen, we might as well
tell Mr. Keller. He'll read about it tomorrow— [ELLEN
rises; crosses to TOMMY.] I told Michael I was going to
read something to one of my English classes and he got
a mistaken idea about it and wrote a sort of—

[CLEOTA *serving coffee.*]

ELLEN. [*Coming down, breaking in quickly.*] Just a silly
little editorial—that's all.

ED. I see.

PATRICIA. [*From fireplace bench.*] Because Tommy isn't
really going to read it at all.

[MYRTLE *rises. Exits up Right carrying plate of food.*]

ED. What was it this kid said, you were going to read? Anything important?

TOMMY. [*After a moment.*] It's a short, but beautifully written piece of English by Bartolomeo Vanzetti.

ED. Never heard of him. [*Takes coffee from* CLEOTA. *Pause.*] Hey, you don't mean Vanzetti of Sacco and Vanzetti!

TOMMY. Yes, the same man.

ED. You mean you're going to read something *he* wrote?

TOMMY. Yes, I was going to.

ELLEN. [*Quickly.*] But now he's not— Michael didn't understand.

ED. Why would you ever think of such a dumb thing in the first place?

TOMMY. It's part of a series. I read many such letters to my class. [*Rises; crosses up. Puts dish table above Right settee.*]

[ELLEN *crosses to up Left Center.*]

ED. You mean letters by anarchists?

TOMMY. [*Restrains himself.*] No, letters by men who were not professional writers—like Lincoln, General Sherman—

ED. Well, it's a good thing you changed your mind. Putting Lincoln and General Sherman in a class with Vanzetti! Wouldn't look very good.

JOE. [*From Center.*] What's this?

ED. [*To* JOE.] Wait a minute. [*To* TOMMY.] Is this thing going to be printed? This editorial?

DAMON. [*Crossing down a step.*] We discovered it too late to stop it.

ED. And this kid didn't submit it to the Publications Committee?

DAMON. Unfortunately, he did not. [*Moves up Center to* ELLEN.] Ellen dear, Mrs. Damon and I must be running along.

ELLEN. Oh, I'm sorry.

DAMON. I have a committee meeting.

BLANCHE. What committee?

DAMON. [*Crossing up.*] Come, Blanche.

BLANCHE. [*Rising.*] Oh, yes, that little committee.

[*They move up to get their hats and coats,* ELLEN *goes up to help them.*]

ED. Well, I hope this thing's not too bad. You better deny it quick, Turner. I tell you. I'll call the papers in the morning.

TOMMY. No, I'll take care of it.

[*He moves upstage as* MYRTLE *enters from dining room with two dishes of sherbet.*]

JOE. What's going on here? [*Rises; crosses downstage.*]

MYRTLE. [*Enters from dining room; crossing down Right.*] Here's some sherbet, Ed.

ED. [*Indicates down Right table.*] Put it down there.

[*She puts it on table and sits Right end of Right settee.*]
I'm just telling Turner here we've had enough of this
Red business among the students and the faculty. Don't
want any more.

TOMMY. [*Sits sofa Center.*] This isn't Red, Mr. Keller.

ED. Maybe not, but it looks bad. We don't want anything
Red—or even Pink—taught here.

[DAMON *puts on coat.*]

TOMMY. But who's to decide what is Red or what is
Pink?

ED. We are! Somebody's got to decide what's fit to teach.
If we don't, who would?

[ELLEN *crosses Center.* DAMON *and* BLANCHE *move
downstage.*]

DAMON. I thought the faculty had—

ED. No sir. You fellows are too wishy-washy. We saw
that in the Chapman case. Americanism is what we want
taught here.

[DAMONS *move up;* DAMON *gets hat.*]

JOE. Americanism is a fine thing.

TOMMY. Fine! But how would you define Americanism?

ED. Why—er—everybody knows what Americanism is!
What do you believe in?

TOMMY. I believe that a college should be concerned with
ideas. Not just your ideas or my ideas, but all ideas.

ED. [*Drowning him out.*] No, sir! That's the *trouble*—

too many ideas floating around— You put ideas of any kind into young people's heads, and the first thing you know, they start believing them.

DAMON. [*Coming down, at* JOE.] On the contrary. I have been putting ideas into young people's heads for forty-two years with no [*Twinkles slyly at* JOE.]—visible—results whatever.

[*There is a dubious laugh from* ED *and* JOE *until* JOE *gets* DAMON'S *meaning.*]

BLANCHE. Come, Frederick. Good night, Ellen! Lovely party! [*She bustles* DAMON *out up Left.*]

ED. [*Rises. Crossing to* TOMMY.] Turner, you better think twice before you read anything. I can promise you the trustees will clamp down on any professor who tries anything funny. I'm telling you that for your own good.

JOE. Say, I thought we were going to have some fun. Let's break this up. How about some music? [*Crosses down Left to Victrola. He puts on a record which starts to play Wayne King's recording of "Cornsilk."*]

ED. That's right. We're celebrating tonight. Just wanted to get that out of my system. [*Crosses Right, sits on settee. He picks up the dish of ice.*] Oh, I didn't want this —I wanted some of that ice cream. [*Rises. He starts for the dining room.*]

MYRTLE. He means he wants both. Here, I'll show you. [*She follows him into the dining room.*]

PATRICIA. [*At a sign from* ELLEN.] I'll bet you'd like some ice cream, too, Mr. Ferguson.

JOE. No, I— [PATRICIA *winks at him; he glances at*

TOMMY.] Oh, sure! Sure, I would. [*He follows* PATRICIA *into dining room.*]

PATRICIA. [*As they exit.*] Can you still skip?

JOE. No—not at my age.

[TOMMY *crosses up Right.*]

ELLEN. Tommy, have you had too much to drink?

TOMMY. No. Not enough.

ELLEN. Your eyes have that funny look.

TOMMY. [*Crossing down Center.*] Did you hear what Mr. Keller said to me? I don't like to be talked to like that.

ELLEN. [*Crossing to him.*] Just because he was nasty and you've had a few drinks. Tommy, you're not going to go ahead and read that letter.

TOMMY. Yes, Ellen, I think I have to.

ELLEN. Tommy, try to be practical for once. At least wait until you're not so mad. Try to think of this the way any other man would think of it.

TOMMY. I'm not any other man.

ELLEN. Well, try to be. Do you think Joe would do something that would get him into trouble just because somebody irritated him?

TOMMY. *Joe!* I don't see why you don't try to understand how *I* feel about this.

ELLEN. I'm simply trying to keep you out of a lot of trouble. I don't see why—

TOMMY. But you see how Joe would feel. That's very plain to you, isn't it?

ELLEN. Yes, it is. Joe wouldn't get all mixed up.

TOMMY. I'm not mixed up. I'm trying to understand what goes on in your mind. It *can't* be like Joe Ferguson's mind!

ELLEN. Oh, you and your mind! I have to go through such a lot with your mind! [*Crossing down Right.*]

TOMMY. Maybe you wouldn't if you understood it better.

ELLEN. [*Turns; crosses back to him.*] Oh, I know, I know! I'm too dumb for you!

TOMMY. [*Crossing Right to Center.*] Now, Ellen, I didn't say that.

ELLEN. [*Crossing Left to Center.*] You said Joe and I were stupid.

TOMMY. I said he was.

ELLEN. But he isn't. He's a big man. In some ways he's smarter than you.

TOMMY. [*Crossing below* ELLEN *to down Right.*] Well, you ought to know.

ELLEN. Oh, look, Tommy—what are we fighting about?

TOMMY. [*Turns.*] You said I was dumb.

ELLEN. Tommy, you've had too many drinks or you wouldn't say that.

TOMMY. No, I haven't, but I don't feel very well. I feel very unhappy and slightly sick.

ELLEN. I'll get you some bicarbonate of soda. [*Starts up.*]

TOMMY. No, you won't. I'll go upstairs and lie down for a few minutes myself. I can do that much. Let's not bring this down to the level of bicarbonate of soda. [*Crosses to stairway—starts up slowly. Suddenly can contain himself no longer—makes a mad dash for it.*]

ELLEN. [*Hesitates for a minute at the foot of the stairs —calls after him.*] Tommy! Tommy, I didn't—

JOE. [*Enters from up Right.*] Anything the matter?

[CLEOTA *enters up Right. Crosses down Right, straightening up the room.*]

ELLEN. Oh—no. Tommy's not feeling well. He got sick once before at a party. He's not used to drinking, and he's very sensitive about it. Cleota. Will you get Mr. Turner some bicarbonate of soda from the kitchen? [CLEOTA *nods—exits up Right.* JOE *crosses down Left to Victrola.*] Cleota will get him some bicarbonate of soda from the kitchen. He'd never find it upstairs.

JOE. [*Turns off the MUSIC and takes off the record.*] Why wouldn't he? Where do you keep it?

ELLEN. In the medicine chest.

JOE. [*Smiles.*] What was that stuff between him and Ed?

ELLEN. Oh, it's nothing, really. I'll tell you about it to-morrow.

JOE. [*Finds another record.*] Fine— Say, look what I found! "Who?" Remember that, Ellen? [*He puts the record on, starts it.*]

[ELLEN *moves closer to the Victrola and listens as it plays:*]

> "Who-o-o stole my heart away?
> Who-o-o makes me dream all day?
> Dreams I know can never come true.
> Seems as though I'd ever be blue
> Who-o-o means my happiness—"

[*As naturally as if they were always dancing to this song, they* BOTH *begin to dance.*] Gee, this takes me back — The May Dance. Remember? [*They are dancing Center.*]

ELLEN. Um-huh—it rained.

JOE. You said you didn't know it was raining. I know I didn't. [*Holds her closer.*]

ELLEN. [*Breaks away.*] I'm a little rusty, Joe. I haven't danced in—oh, I don't remember when. Makes me feel young.

JOE. Then what are we stopping for? Come on.

ELLEN. [*Center.*] Well—all right.

[*They go back into the dance.* JOE *gets her Center and stops, so that they stand looking at each other, he ardently, she caught up in the music.*]

JOE. I can answer all those questions— [*As the music goes into the instrumental reprise,* JOE *kisses her, and she kisses back for a long moment, then tries to pull away.*] No one but you—

ELLEN. [*As he tries to kiss her again.*] Oh, no, Joe, please, I— Say, how many cocktails did *I* have?

[*They stand for an instant, looking at each other. Off-stage we hear:*]

MYRTLE. Ed, get away from that ice cream. You've had enough.

[JOE *and* ELLEN *quietly start dancing again.*]

ED. Oh—all right.

[TOMMY *has come down the stairs—sees them dancing there as* MYRTLE *and* ED *enter up Right.*]

MYRTLE. [*Nudging* ED. JOE *and* ELLEN *dance up Left* JOE *facing stage.*] Look, Ed! Just like the old days, isn't it? Seeing them dancing together?

ED. I'll say. [*Then, loudly.*] They make a darn handsome couple, don't they?

[TOMMY, *although he has not seen the kiss, has sensed the whole intimacy of the scene and the meaning of* ED'S *remark.*]

JOE. She dances like a dream.

ED. [*Chuckling, crossing Right.*] Like a "dream can never come true," eh, Joe? You look mighty sweet in there, boy.

[ELLEN *sees* TOMMY. *Following her glance,* ED *and* MYRTLE *and* JOE *turn and look at* TOMMY.]

ELLEN. [*Breaking away.*] Oh—Tommy—are you all right?

TOMMY. [*Coming down.*] Yes, thanks.—Don't—let me spoil the party.

ED. Party's breaking up anyway, Tommy.

[JOE *crosses down Left, turns off Victrola.*]

TOMMY. I just thought I'd get some more air— [*Crosses to door down Right.*]

ED. [*Crossing up Left.*] I don't want to miss any of that rally. [*A BAND is heard in the distance, approaching. Holds out* MYRTLE'S *coat.*] Myrtle!

[MYRTLE *goes up Left to him.*]

PATRICIA. [*Enters from dining room with bicarbonate of soda in glass.*] Who's this for, Ellen?

[ED *and* JOE *are getting their hats,* JOE *getting* ELLEN'S *coat for her.*]

ELLEN. Tommy! [*To* TOMMY, *as he stands with his back turned, breathing the fresh air.*] Tommy, will you take this bicarbonate?

TOMMY. Just—put it by for a moment. You go to the rally, Ellen— I'm going to walk around out here—and cool off. Good night, everybody— You're coming to lunch tomorrow, aren't you, Joe?

JOE. Yes, sir!

TOMMY. That's what I thought. [*He goes out, down Right, closing the screen door.*]

[ELLEN *puts soda on table.*]

PATRICIA. [*Looks out the window; the BAND is heard louder, coming down.*] Ellen! It's the team and the band and a lot of the kids! They must be going in the Neil Avenue gate! [*Runs back to window.*]

ED. Come on, let's step on it! [*Opens door up Left.*]

[*BAND noise louder.*]

JOE. Yeh. [*Listens to music coming closer.*] Boy, that sounds good! Gosh, doesn't that take you back? [*Gets coat.*]

MYRTLE. [*Up Left getting coat.*] Where'll we go after the rally? [*Crosses down Left Center.*]

JOE. I'll take you all to the Dixie Club! Whatta ya say, Ellen?

ELLEN. Oh, I haven't been there in years! It would be fun— But, no, I'm not going. [*Calls to off down Right.*] I'm going to stay here and get you to bed, Tommy.

TOMMY'S VOICE. [*Off.*] No, I'd rather you didn't— really.

PATRICIA. [*As MUSIC gets much louder.*] Hey! They're stopping in front of the house!

WALLY. [*Enters up Left. Crosses down Right Center.*] Ready, Pat?

PATRICIA. Sure!

WALLY. [*Crossing to* JOE. *He is breathless and excited.*] Look, Mr. Ferguson, we brought the band over to escort you to the chapel. You're going to ride in the Axline Buggy! We hauled it out of the trophy rooms!

[*MUSIC stops at end of piece.*]

ED. The Axline Buggy! Wow!

WALLY. Yes! We got two horses—not the old black ones, but we got two horses! Whatta ya say?

ED. Fine! Fine!

[*WARN Curtain*]

NUTSY. [*Runs in, dressed in band-leader's uniform and carrying his glistening stick. From up Left, by door.*] Hey, come on! Let's get going! The carriage waits, Mr. Ferguson! [*Does drum major's salute and clicks heels.*]

WALLY. [*Pointing to* NUTSY.] This is Nutsy Miller, the leader of the band.

JOE. [*Walks to* NUTSY.] Hiya, Nutsy?

NUTSY. [*Waves a salute.*] Hiya, Joe?

JOE. Okay, fellas! Whatta ya say, Ellen—you ride with me.—Some fun, huh?

ELLEN. [*In the spirit of it.*] Oh—all right. Hurray!

JOE. [*Puts coat around her.*] Hit her, Ed!

ED, JOE, WALLY, ELLEN, PATRICIA, NUTSY. [*Sing.*]
"And if we win the game,
We'll buy a keg of booze,
And we'll drink to old Midwestern
Till we wobble in our shoes."

[*They* ALL *go out,* JOE *and* ELLEN *the center of the gay, excited group, arm in arm. A shout goes up as* JOE *appears outside.*]

VOICES. [*Outside.*]
Oh, we don't give a damn
For the whole state of Michigan
The whole state of Michigan
The whole state of Michigan
Oh, we don't give a damn

For the whole state of Michigan
Now or ever more.
Rah-rah-rah-rah. Ferguson—Ferguson—Ferguson.

[*The BAND starts another march.* TOMMY *has reappeared in the lower Right door a moment after the general exit. He crosses slowly, absently picking up soda on the way, looks out after them, then closes the door. The cheers for Ferguson and the BAND music slowly die away as* TOMMY *comes down, muttering: "Rah. Rah. Rah." He looks at the soda in distaste; distaste for himself. Glances at Victrola, switches it on, dropping needle about twelve bars from the end of the chorus. Victrola plays:*]

"Dreams I know can never come true.
Seems as though I'll always be blue.
Who-o-o means my happiness?
Who-o-o? Shall I answer yes?
Who-o-o? Well, you ought to guess.
Who? Who? No one but you."

[TOMMY *listens for a moment, then makes awkwardly, solemnly, a couple of dance steps, frowns, shakes his head, and drops into settee Left giving it up. He drinks the bitter cup of soda as the MUSIC ends and*]

THE CURTAIN FALLS

ACT TWO

Scene I

Same as Act One. About 1:00 P. M., the following day.
At Rise: JOE, *with coat off, is Center, arranging plates,*
knives, forks, etc., on the floor in the form of a football
team's backfield. The end table has been moved below
the down Right settee and has evidently been used for
serving luncheon as there are still a plate, cup, etc. ELLEN
is seated Center, finishing her coffee and watching JOE.
PATRICIA *is down on her knees on the floor, Left Center*
studying the array of dishes, napkins, salt cellars and
glasses which are ankle-deep around JOE *in football for-*
mation. CLEOTA *enters from the dining room, carrying*
an empty tray. She crosses to the end table down Right,
begins clearing away the dishes.

JOE. Now here—it's a balanced line. Move those two
men out a little more. [PATRICIA *moves men out.*] This
is a wonderful play. [*Jumps downstage facing up. Puts*
downstage "backfield" in position.]

ELLEN. Cleota, did you phone Mr. Turner's office again?

CLEOTA. [*At end table clearing away dishes.*] Yessum.
Dey ain' no answeh.

PATRICIA. I saw Tommy, Ellen—about an hour ago.

ELLEN. Where?

PATRICIA. He was walking out on the little road back of the Ag buildings. Just moping along. I yelled at him, but he didn't hear me.

[JOE *is counting men on the floor.*]

ELLEN. I'm getting worried.

JOE. [*Intent on his own activity.*] Everything's going to be okay. Nothing to worry about— Now, study this play, girls, or you won't know it when you see it this afternoon. [*Points to downstage team.*] This is Michigan. [*Points to upstage team then jumps up.*] And this is Midwestern.—Now! From the balanced line, we shift. Hup! [*He executes a Notre Dame shift.*] Wally takes the left end's place, but he plays out a little.

PATRICIA. [*Exchanges cup and cream pitcher.* CLEOTA *moves to above table Right.*] Isn't Wally going to carry the ball?

JOE. Shh! Michigan spreads out. They're watching that wide end, but it's too obvious. They're watching the other side of the line, too.

CLEOTA. [*Who has moved up Right, comes down.*] What's goin' on heah?

ELLEN. Shh! It's a football game.

JOE. The ball is snapped back. Now look, here we go! Both of us. [*Carrying a plate and a napkin up Left.*] Close together. Fading back but threatening a left end run as well as a pass.

PATRICIA. But who are you?

JOE. I'm both of them—Lindstrom and Wierasocka.— [*Comes forward.*] Skolsky cuts down the left side line

deep and takes out Wupperman—that's the jam pot.
[*Indicates down Left. Picks up "Wally."*] Wally is running wide around right end. [*Runs around down Right.*]
faking as though he had the ball but hasn't really got it
—apparently! [*At down Right.*] Now, then, just as
Michigan is charging in on Lindstrom and Wierasocka,
[*Crosses up Center.*] trying to decide which one has the
ball, Wally lets himself out! *He's really* got it!

PATRICIA. Hooray!

JOE. It's a fake fake. It's an old play, so corny only a
football genius like Coach Sprague would use it. With
no interference at all, Wally cuts over and goes straight
down the right side of the field! He stiff-arms the safety
man— [*Running with the cream pitcher, around Right,
he ends up down Center back to audience.*] Touchdown!

PATRICIA. Whoopee! [*She knocks over the jam pot.*]
Oh, Lord, there goes Wupperman!

[*During* JOE'S *"touchdown,"* TOMMY *has appeared
quietly in door down Right. He watches* JOE *with distaste. No one notices him in the confusion.*]

CLEOTA. Um-hm. You through playin' now?

[PAT *and* JOE *help her pick up dishes, working with backs
to* TOMMY.]

PATRICIA. I'm sorry, Ellen.

ELLEN. It's all right. You can take the teams to the
showers now, Cleota. Can't she, Joe?

JOE. Sure! How do you like it?

[PATRICIA *and* CLEOTA *carry dishes up to sofa and pile
them on tray.*]

ELLEN. I think it's nice. [*Puts cup on up Center table; crosses up to window.*]

JOE. Nice?! It's marvelous! That play is going to put us in the Rose Bowl. [*He puts dishes on down Right table. To* PATRICIA.] Did I ever tell you about how we used the Statue of Liberty play? [*Assumes attitude down Right.*] I would go back for a pass, and Jonesy would take it out of my hand and cut around to the left.

[CLEOTA *picks up tray of dishes and exits up Right. Suddenly* JOE *realizes that, not the imaginary ball but the cup, has been taken out of his hand and that there is no Jonesy. He looks around slowly, puzzled, too late to have seen* TOMMY *quietly returning to the outdoors with the cup. DOORBELL rings.*]

ELLEN. [*Crosses to door Left.*] I'll answer it. [*Admits* DAMON *and they ad lib. in doorway.*]

[JOE *looks to see where he might have dropped the cup; he is still puzzled.*]

PATRICIA. [*Starting for the stairs.*] It's a wonderful play, Mr. Ferguson. If it works. [*Exits up stairs.*]

JOE. The coach gave it to me in strictest confidence. [*Gives another look for cup—repeats gesture with right arm drawn back and lifted, trying to re-live the scene.*]

[ELLEN *and* DAMON *have been ad libbing up Left.*]

ELLEN. Can you come in and wait, Doctor Damon? Tommy is out somewhere, but I'm expecting him back.

[CLEOTA *exits with tray and dishes, leaving coffee things on Right table.*]

DAMON. [*Crossing down to Left.*] I can't wait very long. [*Indicates magazine in pocket.*]

ELLEN. [*Following him.*] Is that *The Literary Magazine?*

DAMON. It's a powder magazine. [*Coming down Center.*] Bombs are bursting all around. [*Sees* JOE, *who has been putting on coat and looking in drapes for cup.*] Oh —good afternoon.

JOE. Good afternoon, Doctor Damon.

[*PHONE rings.*]

ELLEN. Excuse me, I'll— [*She goes to phone—picks up receiver.* DAMON *moves down Left Center.* JOE *is still looking for the vanished cup, moving drapes slightly.*] Hello— Yes, thank you. [*Hangs up.*] That was Ed Keller's office, Joe. He's on his way over here.

JOE. Oh, yeah. He called me this morning. He's fit to be tied about this *Literary Magazine* thing. Have you seen it?

DAMON. [*From down Left Center.*] Yes. This is it.

JOE. [*Crossing to* DAMON.] May I take a look at it? Gosh, I didn't realize what this thing was— [*He takes magazine and scans editorial.*] Calls the trustees Fascists! This kid's dangerous—un-American.

DAMON. Oh, no!

ELLEN. [*Crossing to* JOE. *At same time.*] Oh, no, not really. He's from an old Chillicothe family.

JOE. This is bad stuff for the university. I'm afraid all hell's going to break loose. Of course, it's none of my business, but—

DAMON. [*Taking the magazine out of* JOE's *hand.*] You take the words right out of my mouth. I haven't had such a day since poor Doctor Prendergast shot his secretary. [*Crosses and sits down Left settee.*]

JOE. Well, I'm not a trustee, but I know how they feel.

ELLEN. I know. [*Crosses to down Right Center.*]

JOE. Tommy'd better deny this, pretty fast, and get himself out in the clear. I'm telling you. [*Crosses to* ELLEN.] I'm sorry about this, Ellen— Where is Tommy?

ELLEN. I don't know.

JOE. You don't think— [*Lowers voice to whisper.*] You don't think he may be a little sore about your going out with me last night?

ELLEN. I don't know. Oh, Joe, I'm all upset.

[*DOORBELL rings.*]

JOE. Shall I answer it?

ELLEN. Would you?

JOE. [*He opens door.*] Hi, Ed!

ED. [*In doorway.*] Turner here?

ELLEN. No, he isn't.

ED. Well, I want to see him before the game. Tell him to call my office. Coming, Joe?

ELLEN. [*Quickly.*] I don't know just when he'll— Won't you come in? Dean Damon is here.

ED. Oh! [*He comes into the room a few steps.* JOE *closes the door.* ED *crosses down to* DAMON.] Well. I'm glad somebody's here. How do you do, sir? Do you know where I could find President Cartwright?

DAMON. His secretary informed me that he is at the barber shop, having his beard trimmed.

ED. That'll be a big help! [*To* ELLEN, *then* JOE.] I thought Turner was going to deny this story. Papers keep calling *me*—they say he hasn't. Here I am, bearing the brunt of this damn disgraceful attack. "Fascists!" You oughtta heard Si McMillan! And do you know Kressinger's in town from Detroit? [*Crosses down Left Center.*]

ELLEN. Is he a trustee, too?

DAMON. Oh, yes, young Michael certainly exploded his dynamite at a moment when the concentration of trustees is at its thickest.

ED. [*Crossing Center.*] Yeh. There goes the new stadium. There goes your Endowment Fund! Unless something is done, and done quick! [*Crossing to* ELLEN.] Ellen, you tell your husband what I said!

JOE. [*Moving in.*] Look, Ed, it isn't Ellen's fault.

ED. [*Crossing to* JOE.] It isn't my fault, either. Here, I kept this whole week-end free. I've got my office full of eighteen-year-old Bourbon so we fellows could cut loose a little. And look what happens! All we need now is for Wierasocka to fumble a punt! [*Stomps out up Left.*]

JOE. I'll—see you later. [*Takes overcoat and hat up Left; follows* ED *out.*]

DAMON. I didn't like the way Mr. Keller said "There

goes your Endowment Fund." [*PHONE rings.*] If that's the newspapers I'm not here.

ELLEN. [*Rises—going toward phone.*] Oh, I don't want to talk to them either. [*Goes to dining-room door. Calls.*] Cleota—

[*PHONE rings again.*]

PATRICIA. [*Runs down the stairs.*] I'm going out to talk to Michael. [*Runs into* ELLEN.] I got him on the phone but he hung up on me! [*PHONE rings. Crossing Left.*] Good afternoon, Doctor Damon. [*Gets coat up Left.*] I'll knock his ears off. [*Slams out the Left door.*]

[*PHONE rings.*]

DAMON. [*Calling after her.*] Good afternoon, Patricia.

[CLEOTA *enters from the dining room.*]

ELLEN. Answer the phone, Cleota.

CLEOTA. [*Crosses to phone.*] Hello— Says what?—Says he is?—Ah didn' say you said he was, I say what is it? —No, he ain' heah— No, dis ain' Miz Turner.

ELLEN. [*Prompting her.*] *Who is calling, please.*

CLEOTA. Who's dis?—Wait a minute— [*Puts hand over mouthpiece—to* ELLEN.] It's de *Daily* sump'n.

ELLEN. Hang up, Cleota.

CLEOTA. G'bye. [*Hangs up and exits up Right.*]

ELLEN. [*Crossing to* DAMON.] Oh, Lord, see what's happened already! Doctor Damon, suppose Tommy didn't read this letter?

DAMON. Let us not take refuge in conditional clauses, my dear.

ELLEN. Would you read it if you were Tommy?

DAMON. Now we go into the subjunctive. My dear, for forty-two years I have read nothing to my classes which was written later than the first half of the seventeenth century.

ELLEN. [*Turns up Left Center.*] There must be some way—some compromise—that wouldn't be too humiliating.

DAMON. The policy of appeasement? Yes, it has its merits, and I'm afraid it's all I have to offer. [*Rises. Crossing to* ELLEN.] I can't wait any longer for Thomas. Tell him that if he decides not to read the letter, I shall feel easier in my mind. Much easier. [*Picks up hat. Comes back.*] And—slightly disappointed— Good afternoon, my dear— [*He opens the door, and in flies* PATRICIA. *They collide.* ELLEN *moves Right Center.*] Wup, wup, *wup!*

PATRICIA. Don't let Michael in! I don't want to talk to him any more! [*Crossing Right a few steps.*]

DAMON. Did you—uh—knock his ears off?

PATRICIA. [*Turns to* DAMON.] I got him told. But he wants to tell me his side of it. He thinks *he* has a side.

DAMON. A common failing, my dear— Good afternoon [*He goes out up Left.*]

PATRICIA. [*Bolts the door after him.*] There, I've bolted that young genius out! [*Crossing to* ELLEN.] Oh, Ellen! Give me a football player any time. [*Crossing down*

Left Center.] Give me a guy without so much intellect or whatever it is. Somebody that doesn't want to be bawling the world out all the time—always doing something brave or fine or something. [*Turns as* MICHAEL *comes in down Right slamming door.*] Go away!

ELLEN. Quiet down, Patricia— Come in, Michael.

MICHAEL. [*Down Right. To* PATRICIA.] You're being very silly.

ELLEN. [*Noticing* MICHAEL'S *distraught look.*] Can I give you a glass of milk?

MICHAEL. No, thank you. She won't listen to me, Mrs. Turner. I'm not trying to ruin your husband's life or my life or anybody's life. It's the principle of the thing she won't see.

PATRICIA. Oh, the principle! [*Crossing to Right Center.*] I'll bet nobody else would make a fool of himself and his friends and—my brother-in-law—over a principle.

[ELLEN, *taking the dishes with her, quietly slips out toward the kitchen, unnoticed by* MICHAEL.]

MICHAEL. [*With the enormous gravity of the young man in love. Crossing Left to* PATRICIA.] All right, Pat. I'm very glad to know the qualities you admire in a man. They are certainly the noble virtues, and I'm sure Wally is lousy with them.

PATRICIA. Oh, make up your mind who you're imitating, Ralph Waldo Emerson or Hemingway! You—you *writer!* [*Crosses below* MICHAEL *to down Right.*]

MICHAEL. [*Turns.*] Now who's imitating Hemingway?

PATRICIA. [*Turns to him.*] I wish you'd go away! [*Starts for door down Right.*]

MICHAEL. [*Crossing to up Left door.*] I'm going! [*Goes to door, places hand on knob, turns.* PATRICIA *stops, turns, watches him.*] I'm going for good! I'm going out of your life! [*On the last word he jerks at door to make a dramatic exit, but it won't open, since* PAT *bolted it. Doorknob comes off in his hand.*]

PATRICIA. [*With a smile of complete victory.*] It's bolted, you dope! [*Exits down Right.*]

[MICHAEL *inserts knob and gets the door open finally. In walks* TOMMY *with the other doorknob in his hand. The two stand and look at each other. The knob has again come out in* MICHAEL'S *hand.*]

MICHAEL. [*A little guiltily.*] Sorry, Mr. Turner!

TOMMY. What's going on here?

[MICHAEL *puts the knob in.* TOMMY *screws the other knob on.*]

MICHAEL. I was just going.

TOMMY. That's all right. Come in if you want to.

MICHAEL. Say, you look terrible.

TOMMY. Me? Why, what's the matter?

MICHAEL. I've got to get out of here.

TOMMY. [*Shuts door.*] Oh, it's all right, Michael. Come in. Did somebody do something to you? [*Crossing Center.*]

MICHAEL. Patricia. She did plenty. I suppose it's just as

well. I've found out what she wants in life: a handsome, half-witted half-back.

TOMMY. [*Crossing to foot of stairs and looking up.*] Yes, I know how that feels.

MICHAEL. Yes, sir. Well, you can't get anywhere with a woman who doesn't understand what you have to do.

TOMMY. [*Crosses to* MICHAEL.] No. No, you can't, Michael. You'd like to, but you can't— Well— Good-bye, Michael— Come back in about an hour, will you? I want to give you a piece of my mind.

MICHAEL. [*Puzzled.*] Yes, sir. [*Exits up Left.*]

[TOMMY *looks around—takes cup out of pocket and puts it on table up Center; hangs up coat and hat up Left, then crosses to settee Left and sits thinking.*]

ELLEN. [*Enters up Right.*] Oh, hello, darling!

TOMMY. Hello!

ELLEN. [*Crossing to him.*] Well, I'm glad you remembered where you live. I was beginning to be worried. We phoned your office three times, but nobody knew where you were.

TOMMY. [*Looking up slowly.*] Huh?

ELLEN. I say nobody knew where you were—since early this morning.

TOMMY. I was walking.

ELLEN. Without any breakfast? All this time?

TOMMY. [*Rises. Crosses down Left.*] Well, I—came around to the back door a while ago, but Joe was doing the Statue of Liberty or something again, so I went away.

ELLEN. You were right here and you went away?

TOMMY. [*Crosses down Right.*] Yes, I couldn't face that right now. Not the Statue of Liberty.

ELLEN. Oh! Well, Doctor Damon's been here—and Ed Keller, and the newspapers have been calling up. There's going to be a lot of trouble if you don't hurry up and deny that story of Michael's—or have you done it?

TOMMY. No—I haven't denied it.

ELLEN. [*Center. Troubled.*] You mean you've made up your mind to read it? Is that what you've been—walking around for? Tommy, I don't know what to say to you.

TOMMY. [*Turns. Crosses to her.*] I think maybe you've said enough already.

ELLEN. That isn't very kind.

TOMMY. None of this is going to sound very kind but I've figured out exactly what I want to say, and I have to get it out before I get all mixed up.

ELLEN. I don't see why you are being so mean.

TOMMY. It's just that last night I began to see you, and myself, clearly for the first time. [*Crosses above* ELLEN *up Left.*]

ELLEN. [*Turns downstage.*] If this is a story you're writing, and you're trying it out on me, it isn't very good.

TOMMY. Oh, I saw you and Joe clearly, too.

ELLEN. [*Relieved. Crossing to* TOMMY *a little.*] Oh, you saw him kiss me— I thought that was it—

TOMMY. [*Covering.*] No—No, I didn't—Did he kiss you? Well, that's fine—I've been meaning to ask you, what became of Housman's "Last Poems"? [*Turns to Left bookcase.*]

ELLEN. [*Crossing up to* TOMMY.] Tommy, [*Puts her hand on his shoulder.*] listen to me—I wanted to have a good time last night, and you spoiled it—

TOMMY. [*Turns to her.*] Didn't you enjoy it at all?

ELLEN. [*Piqued.*] Yes, I did. [*Crossing Right two steps.*] I'm not a hundred years old—yet. I just decided to quit worrying about you, and have a little fun. For about an hour I felt like a girl again—wearing flowers at a Spring Dance—when I was young and silly—

TOMMY. Young and happy.

ELLEN. [*Turns to* TOMMY.] All right, he—kissed me. I kissed him, too. [*Crossing to* TOMMY.] We didn't go out in the dark to do it.

TOMMY. [*Piling books he is taking from book shelves on down Left settee.*] I hope you didn't lend that book to anybody; it was a first edition.

ELLEN. Did *you* hear what *I* said?

TOMMY. Sure, I heard you. I'm listening— You said you went out in the dark and kissed Joe.

ELLEN. [*Turns. Crossing to down Right Center.*] I said no such thing, and you know it.

TOMMY. [*Still at bookcase.*] I wish we had had separate book-plates.

ELLEN. [*Turns to him.*] So that when you really make me mad and I get out of here, I can find my own books quickly?

TOMMY. [*At bookcase.*] I hate sentimental pawing over things by a couple breaking up. We're not living in the days of Henry James and Meredith. Look at Joe and his wife.

ELLEN. Tommy, [*Crossing Left to up Left Center.*] I want you to stop this. If you're going to be jealous *be* jealous, rave or throw things, but don't act like the lead in a Senior Class play! [*This thrust gets home.*]

TOMMY. [*Up Left.*] I'm trying to tell you that I don't care what you and Joe do. I'm trying to tell you that it's fine. It's very lucky that he came back just now.

ELLEN. What do you mean?

TOMMY. I mean on the money *I* make, I can go on fine alone, reading whatever I want to to my classes. That's what I want. And that's what I'm going to do.

ELLEN. Oh, that's what you want! Suddenly that's what you want. More than me?

TOMMY. It isn't so sudden. [*Crossing Right.*] Not any more sudden than your feeling for Joe. It's logical. We get in each other's way. You wear yourself out picking up after me. Taking matches out of my pockets. [*Finds matches in pockets and throws them on table Right.*] Disarranging my whole way of life. [*Sits on down Right settee.*]

ELLEN. [*Follows him to chair Right Center.*] Why haven't you said all this before?

TOMMY. I couldn't very well.

ELLEN. Why couldn't you? If you felt this way?

TOMMY. Well, we hadn't split up on this letter issue, for one thing—and then there was no place for you to go. I didn't want you to have to go back to Cleveland, or to work in some tea shoppe.

ELLEN. Oh, I see. Some tea shoppe! That's what you think I'd have to do! [*Crosses up Right.*] Well, you needn't have spared my feelings. I can make as much money as you.

TOMMY. You don't have to, now.

ELLEN. [*Turns.*] Oh, you mean you waited to tell me this till Joe came along! I thought you were jealous of Joe. I could understand that. You aren't the least bit aroused at the idea of his kissing me— [*Crosses downstage, drives this at him.*] out in the dark—for hours!

TOMMY. No, I'm not.

ELLEN. So that's why you've been wandering around! That's what you've been figuring out! How nice it would be if he would take me off your hands, so you could be left alone with your books and match-boxes and *litter!* [*Crosses to Left Center.*] I suppose any man would do as well as Joe. [*Crosses back to TOMMY two steps.*]

TOMMY. [*Crossing to her.*] He's not just any man, and you know that. He's always been in love with you, and you've always been in love with him! [*He is angry and jealous now.*]

ELLEN. [*Crossing Left.*] That's ridiculous!

TOMMY. [*Moving toward her.*] I felt it when I saw you dancing together. It was unmistakable. You've just admitted it.

ELLEN. [*Turns. Crossing to him.*] Oh, you can't do that now! You can't be jealous now just because you think I want you to be!

TOMMY. I saw you dancing together—like angels! [ELLEN *turns away.*] I saw you go out in that carriage together! I saw you together years ago, when I was young enough and dumb enough to believe that I really took you away from him. [ELLEN *turns back.*] There's something that happens when you two dance together that doesn't happen when we dance together!

ELLEN. All right—have it your way. If you want to be free, then I want to be free—and I've gone around for ten years mooning about Joe— Well, maybe I have— maybe I have, because I'm certainly sick of you right now! [*Whirls away from him.*]

TOMMY. [*Shaking her.*] Ellen—Ellen, listen—

ELLEN. Never mind—all right—*all right—ALL RIGHT!* [*She breaks away up Center—suddenly stops short as* JOE *enters Left brightly.*]

JOE. Oh, I'm sorry—if I— [*He stops in embarrassment. There is a pause. He has caught only the tone; but he sees and feels the tension. He is carrying a wrapped bottle and a newspaper. He removes overcoat, lays it on chair up Left.*]

TOMMY [*Crossing down Right.*] Hello, Joe!

JOE. Hello! [*Pause.*] I brought the rum. [*Holds up bottle, sees only their backs. Crosses down to coffee table Left. Puts bottle on table; holds up newspaper.*] Big picture of Wally all over the front page. [*Silence.*] Good picture, isn't it?

TOMMY. You and Ellen have some rum.

JOE. The rum's for the punch—later.

ELLEN. Could I have some—now? [*Sits on sofa up Center.*]

[TOMMY *exits up Right.*]

JOE. [*Surprised.*] Right now?—Sure. [*Unwraps bottle; throws paper in waste-basket up Left.*]

TOMMY. [*From dining room.*] I'll get you some glasses. [*Re-enters—crosses Left to* JOE *with two glasses, then goes above settee Left, glancing at* ELLEN.]

JOE. [*Unscrewing the top.*] Tommy, old man, I just left Ed Keller and Si McMillan. This thing your young friend wrote in the magazine. [*Pours drink.*] I read the piece over again. He's got you on a spot, Tommy. [*Crosses to* ELLEN—*gives her drink.*]

ELLEN. Want to drink a toast, Joe?—To Tommy's happiness?

JOE. [*Looks at both of them—then crosses down Left.*] Sure— [*Pours himself drink—crosses up—offers toast.*] Your happiness, Tommy. [*They drink amid a long silence,* JOE *nervously finishing his;* ELLEN *taking a long drink, grimacing as the drink burns her throat.*] What's the matter? What's it about? Maybe I could talk to Ed—

TOMMY. No. I don't want that. I'll run my own life my own way.

ELLEN. That's what it's about. Tommy wants to—live alone.

JOE. What?

ELLEN. He wants to be left alone—

JOE. I beg your pardon?

ELLEN. Us! Tommy and me! We're breaking up!

JOE. [*Awed, puzzled.*] *Just before the game—?* [TOMMY *puts books from settee down Left on fireplace bench.*] You're both crazy! Maybe I better go.

TOMMY. Not at all! You're not exactly a stranger around here. You knew Ellen as long ago as I did.

JOE. I knew her a long time before you did—and this is a fine way to be treating her.

TOMMY. [*Baiting a hook.*] Yes, I know. I was just saying I barged in and took her away from you.

JOE. Oh, no, you didn't. You had nothing to do with it. She got sore at me on account of another girl.

TOMMY. Oh, that's where I came in?

JOE. Sure! If you think you took her away from me, you're crazy. Here, you better have some rum.

ELLEN. He can't drink this early.

TOMMY. [*Sits settee down Left.*] I don't *need* any rum. Go on, Joe.

JOE. [*Sits Right end of sofa.*] Well, Ellen and I had a fight. You weren't in on it. You came in later—

ELLEN. Joe, do we have to—

TOMMY. It's all right. It's his turn.

JOE. She said she hated me and never wanted to see me again. She threw something at me. She thought I went away with this girl—I mean—

TOMMY. Never mind—I know what you mean—

ELLEN. I never said you went. I never said that.

JOE. Oh, yes, you did—you intimated it.

ELLEN. No, that was your idea. I thought you were bragging about it.

JOE. Well, you got awfully mad. I thought you never did want to see me again. I guess I was dumb. Brenda says it shows you liked me. [*From* ELLEN'S *expression,* JOE *is reminded of* TOMMY'S *presence; he turns.*] Oh—sorry!

TOMMY. Oh, don't mind me. Who's Brenda? Another girl?

JOE. My wife.

TOMMY. Oh, sorry!

JOE. Ellen knows her. She's from Cleveland. Brenda's always been jealous of Ellen. She found a picture of you.

TOMMY. What picture?

ELLEN. I gave him a picture. He wouldn't give it back.

JOE. It's a swell picture. You were wearing that floppy hat. Red.

ELLEN. Blue.

JOE. It had ribbons. Made you look like you were sixteen.

TOMMY. I've never seen it.

ELLEN. It was a silly hat. This was ages ago.

TOMMY. I mean, I've never seen the picture.

ELLEN. [*Angrily.*] I threw them all away.

JOE. [*Remembering.*] It kind of went down over one eye.

TOMMY. She looks nice in hats like that.

[ELLEN *suddenly begins to cry; collapses on sofa.*]

JOE. [*Rising.*] Now look what you've done!

TOMMY. [*Rising.*] Look what *you've* done! Bringing up old floppy blue hats! [JOE *moves to* ELLEN.] Don't touch her! She doesn't like to be touched when she's crying. [*Crosses to Left Center.*]

JOE. I've seen her cry. I know what to do.

TOMMY. Oh, you do?

JOE. She cried when we had that fight about the girl. She was lying on the floor and kicking and crying—on her stomach.

ELLEN. I was not!

TOMMY. Be careful what you say!

JOE. Well, I mean I knew what to do. [*Crosses to other end of sofa.*] I picked her up then.

TOMMY. Well, you're not going to pick her up now. [*Crosses below* JOE.]

ELLEN. Will you both please let me alone?! Will you please go away!

JOE. There! She wants you to go away. And I don't blame her, if this is the way you treat her. I wouldn't have stood for it ten years ago, and I'm not going to stand for it now.

TOMMY. [*Crossing to* JOE *a step.*] But what are you going to do?

JOE. I'm going to get her away from all this! It isn't nice!

TOMMY. It isn't exactly to my taste, either. [*Crossing to up Left end of sofa.*] I didn't want it to turn out this way, but it did: me feeling like a cad, Ellen crying, and you acting like a fool.

JOE. Me acting like a fool?

ELLEN. Everybody's acting like a fool. [*Puts glass up Center table.*]

JOE. [*Crossing down Right Center.*] You've certainly messed things up, brother.

TOMMY. Don't call me brother! [*From up Left Center.*] I can't stand that, now! [*In one step.*]

JOE. If Ellen weren't here, I'd call you worse than brother.

ELLEN. [*Sitting up.*] Well, I'm not going to be here! Please, please, stop—both of you! Nobody has said a word about what *I* want to do. You're going to settle that between yourselves. Bandying me back and forth!

TOMMY. [*Crossing to her.*] Nobody's bandying you, Ellen.

ELLEN. [*Sniffling.*] I know when I'm being bandied!
[*Rises—looks at them.*] I don't want either of you!
You can both go to hell! [*Runs upstairs, crying.*]

TOMMY. [*Up to stairs.* JOE *also crosses to stairs.* BOTH
look up, then each looks away.] She means me.

JOE. She said both of us.

TOMMY. She was looking at me.

JOE. How did we get into this anyway?

TOMMY. You two-stepped into it. You kissed your way
into it.

JOE. [*Crossing down to below Right Center chair.*] I'm
sorry about that. Sorry it happened.

TOMMY. You're not sorry it happened. You're sorry I
found it out. [*Crossing to Left of up Center sofa.*] Do
you know anything about women? [*Crossing to* JOE.]
Didn't you know what she was thinking about when she
was dancing with you?

JOE. No. I don't think when I'm dancing.

TOMMY. I know. You think in your office. Well, you'll
have to think in your home after this. She likes to be
thought about.

JOE. I thought about her. I remembered her birthday.
I brought her flowers.

TOMMY. Well, you'll have to keep on bringing her things
—fur coats and things— She's still young and pretty.

JOE. I don't get you.

TOMMY. I'm being broadminded. [*Crossing Left.*] I'm taking things in my stride. It's the modern way of doing things. You ought to know that.

JOE. [*Shrewdly.*] What makes me think you're still crazy about her and are up to some damn something or other?

TOMMY. Don't be acute. I couldn't stand you being acute. [*Crossing down Left.*]

JOE. I'm not dumb.

TOMMY. [*Turning back to him.*] Yes, you are. [*Crossing Right to* JOE.] It isn't what I feel that counts. It's what she feels. I think she's always been in love with you. Why, I don't know. It's supposed to be beyond reason. I guess it is.

JOE. You just think that because of last night?

TOMMY. No. Because of what lay behind last night. That wasn't just a kiss. That's nothing. [*Crosses up Center, and turns.*] This thing is too deep for jealousy or for anything but honesty. A woman must not go on living with a man when she dances better with another man.

JOE. That's silly. [*Crossing down Right.*] *That's the silliest—* [*Crossing up Left to* TOMMY *up Center.*] Dancing doesn't mean everything.

TOMMY. The way you *do* it does. The things that happen to you. The light you give off.

JOE. *Light?!*

TOMMY. Oh, these things are too subtle for you, Joe. I've made some study of them. [*Turns away.*]

JOE. Maybe all this studying's bad for you.

TOMMY. All I want to know is whether you felt the same thing she felt last night.

JOE. I felt fine. [*Crossing Right.*] This is embarrassing! [*Crossing Left to* TOMMY.] A man makes love to a woman. He doesn't talk it over with her husband!

TOMMY. I'm just trying to be honest.

JOE. [*Crossing below* TOMMY *to down Left.*] You're a funny guy. Conscientious. What does it get you? Like this letter you're going to read— Say, is that what started the trouble?

TOMMY. Yes, it's an integral part of the trouble—things like that.

JOE. [*Sits Right end down Left settee.*] Well, what are we going to do? I mean now? I mean from now on?

TOMMY. From now on will work itself out. Right now you'd better go upstairs and comfort her. She'll be expecting you.

JOE. Oh, no. Not me! You ought to know more what to do right now. It's your house. She's still your wife.

TOMMY. [*Crossing to* JOE.] She doesn't want to talk to me. She's just done that. But she oughtn't to be left alone right now. [JOE *hesitates.*] Well, don't be a big baby!!

JOE. [*Crossing Right to stairs, turns.*] It doesn't seem right somehow for me to go upstairs.

TOMMY. This is not a moment for cheap moralizing!

JOE. Well—good God Almighty! [*Goes upstairs.*]

[TOMMY *looks after* JOE *then sits on sofa up Center.*]

MICHAEL. [*Comes in up Left door as* TOMMY *sighs deeply.*] What's the matter?

TOMMY. [*Sees him.*] Oh! Why don't you knock? Never mind— [*Rises. Crosses down and paces; he glares upstairs, still has his glare when he turns back to* MICHAEL.]

MICHAEL. Well, I came back like you said.

TOMMY. *As* you said. Oh—never mind!

[*The two* MEN *pace, meeting down Right Center.*]

MICHAEL. Before you start in on me, Mr. Turner, please remember that I've been through a lot today. I can't stand much more.

TOMMY. [*Pats him on shoulder.*] Thanks.

MICHAEL. [*At Center. Gloomily.*] They'll probably do something to you—especially if we lose to Michigan. You know what Keller did the last time they beat us in a Homecoming Game? He ran the flag on his office building down to half mast.

TOMMY. [*Looking upstairs—distracted. Crossing around to up Right Center; then to landing.*] Don't worry about me.

MICHAEL. Well, I'm feeling better. I've put her out of my mind. It's ended as simply as that. [*Drops into chair Right Center.*] There's a girl who could sit with you and talk about Shelley. Well, I'm glad I found out about women. [*CRASH upstairs.*] What was that?

TOMMY. I'm sure I don't know. What were you saying? [*Crosses up Center.*]

MICHAEL. I say Patricia knew things. She knew odd things like, "A Sonnet on Political Greatness": [TOMMY *paces up Left Center.*] she quoted that one night. Wouldn't you think a girl like that had some social consciousness?

TOMMY. [*Sits sofa up Center.*] That's the sonnet that ends:
> "Quelling the anarchy of hopes and fears,
> Being himself alone."

MICHAEL. Yes, but when an issue comes up and a man has to be himself alone, she reveals the true stature of her character and goes off to Hennick's with that football player. I saw them—right in the front window—drinking Seven-Up—he uses a straw.

TOMMY. [*Crossing down to* MICHAEL.] Yes, but he's handsome. [*Paces.*] What is more, he whirls. He's a hunter. He comes home at night with meat slung over his shoulders, and you sit there drawing pictures on the wall of your cave. [*Crosses around Left to down Left; then up Center.*]

MICHAEL. I see. Maybe I ought to sock him with a ball bat.

TOMMY. [*Crossing Center.*] No. You are a civilized man, Michael. If the male animal in you doesn't like the full implications of that, he must nevertheless be swayed by Reason. You are not living in the days of King Arthur when you fought for your woman. [*Crossing down Left.*] Nowadays, the man and his wife and the other man talk it over. Quietly and calmly. They all go out to dinner together. [*Sits Right end settee down Left.*]

MICHAEL. Intellectually, Patricia is sleeping with that guy. I feel like going out tonight with the Hot Cha-cha.

TOMMY. With the what?

MICHAEL. It's a girl. They call her that. What if she was kicked out of the Pi Phi House? She's honest! She does what she believes in! And—well, Hot Cha-cha doesn't argue all the time anyway.

TOMMY. Look, Michael, hasn't she got a name? You don't call her *that,* do you?

MICHAEL. Marcia Gardner. They just call her—

TOMMY. Yes, you told me what they call her. [*Slight pause.*]

MICHAEL. [*Transformed.*] Patricia's not coming to class when you read that letter. She's gone over to the Philistines— Oh, Mr. Turner, I wish I were like you! Middle-aged, settled down, happily married— [TOMMY *takes off his glasses and peers across at* MICHAEL.] and through with all this hell you feel when you're young and in love.

TOMMY. [*Nettled.*] Middle-aged?

MICHAEL. Yes, you know what Rupert Brooke says:
          "That time when all is over,

[TOMMY *writhes, turns his back.*]

          And love has turned to kindliness."
Is kindliness peaceful?

TOMMY. Don't ask me. [*Two quick CRASHES from upstairs bring* TOMMY *to his feet as* JOE *enters down the stairs, looking worn and worried, his hair slightly disarranged.* TOMMY *crosses to* JOE. *Sharply.*] You look ruffled!

JOE. [*Just as sharply, but a bit absently.*] *What?*

[*The two* MEN *look each other over.*]

TOMMY. I say—what ruffled you?

JOE. Do we have to discuss these things in front of this boy?

MICHAEL. [*Rising. Crossing to* JOE.] I am not a boy.

TOMMY. This is Michael Barnes. [*Goes up Left Center, looking upstairs.*]

JOE. [*Turning to* MICHAEL.] Oh, so you're the little boy that started all this! I want to tell you that you write too much, you have too much to say, you get too many people into too much trouble. You've not only got Tommy and Ellen involved, but me. [*Gesturing to* TOMMY— *upstairs—to himself.*]

MICHAEL. I don't see how this concerns you, do you, Mr. Turner?

TOMMY. Yes. [*Crosses down to Right end of settee Left.*]

MICHAEL. What?

JOE. [*Waving* MICHAEL *out.*] Goodbye!

MICHAEL. [*In wordless wrath at being treated like a child.*] Oh! [*Exits down Right to garden.*]

JOE. Oh, God, I wish I was in Pittsburgh! [*Sits Right Center chair.*]

TOMMY. [*Eagerly.*] What happened?

JOE. Well, old man, I guess you're right. She was pretty

bitter—about you. She picked up something you'd given her and threw it against the wall and broke it into a thousand pieces.

TOMMY. What was it?

JOE. I didn't see it till after she threw it.

TOMMY. [*Sits sofa up Center*.] Oh!

JOE. Every time she mentioned your name, she threw something. Kept me ducking.

TOMMY. [*Sadly*.] I see. You want to marry Ellen, don't you?

JOE. Well, I always liked her, but I don't like to go through so much. [*Pause*.] Are you sure you understand women?

TOMMY. Yes.

JOE. Well, when Ellen and I had that fight about the girl, she threw things on account of me, and Brenda thinks that meant she was in love with me. Now she throws things on account of *you.*

TOMMY. [*After an instant of hope*.] In both instances, she threw them at *you,* didn't she?

JOE. [*Glumly*.] Yeh, I guess so.

TOMMY. Well, there you are. What did she say when you left? What was she doing?

JOE. She was in a terrible state. I don't think she'll be able to go to the game. She may have a sick headache for days. What do you do then?

TOMMY. Get her a hot water bottle. [*Rises. Crossing up Right to dining room*.] Cleota!—Cleota!

CLEOTA. [*Off.*] Yes, suh?

TOMMY. There's a hot water bottle out there in the—somewhere. [*Returning.*] Fill it and bring it in, please.

CLEOTA. [*Off.*] Yes, suh.

[TOMMY *crosses and sits on sofa up Center.*]

JOE. [*Rises. Glances at wrist-watch. Crossing down Left.*] I don't want to miss this game. I sort of wish Stalenkiwiecz wasn't laid up, don't you? [*Crossing to Center.*]

TOMMY. I haven't given it much thought one way or another.

JOE. [*Crossing down Right.*] Of course, Wierasocka's all right, but Stalenkiwiecz is a better pass-receiver.

TOMMY. Is he? Why?

JOE. [*Turning to* TOMMY.] I don't know why. He just is. "Why!" [*His pacing has carried him to lower door, Right. He remembers the vanishing cup and takes one more look.*] 'Course they may not give Brenda a divorce. [*Crossing Left.*]

TOMMY. I think they will.

JOE. I don't know.

CLEOTA. [*Enters up Right with hot water bottle and folded towel. She hands them to* TOMMY *on up Center sofa.*] Is you gotta pain?

TOMMY. No.—Oh, thank you.

[CLEOTA *exits up Right.*]

JOE. [*Pacing Left.*] I don't suppose we ought to go and leave her.

TOMMY. [*Rises. Going to him with bottle.*] Oh, I'm not going. Here. [*Hands him bottle and towel.*]

JOE. [*Taking it. It burns his hand.*] Ow!

TOMMY. Hold it by the end.

JOE. Won't this thing burn her?

TOMMY. [*Impatiently.*] You wrap the towel around it. [*Places towel around shoulders of bottle. Crosses up Center, then down around Right Center chair to down Right.*]

JOE. You shouldn't stay here in the house alone with her, things being the way they are, should you?

TOMMY. Please don't worry about that!

JOE. [*Looking at the bottle.*] I thought these things were different now than they used to be.

TOMMY. What do you mean, different?

JOE. I mean better looking—somehow.

[*There is a pause during which* JOE *tries to wrap the towel around the hot water bottle but various parts of it insist on remaining exposed. Finally* TOMMY, *who has moved upstage, crosses down to* JOE *angrily.*]

TOMMY. Well, why don't you take it up to her?

ELLEN. [*Coming down the stairs.*] It's time to get started, isn't it? [*The two* MEN *turn and stare at her,* JOE *still holding the hot water bottle.* ELLEN *is utterly serene, with no sign of tears or hysterics. Washed and powdered, with her hat on, she stands at the foot of the stairs, putting on her gloves.*] Do you realize what time it is? The Kellers will be waiting for us at Esther Baker's. We'll leave the car there and walk to the stadium. It's only a block. [*The* MEN *are still staring. She crosses to* JOE.] What are you doing with that thing, Joe?

TOMMY. He was going to lie down with it for a while.

JOE. I was not! Here! [*Tries to hand it to* TOMMY.]

TOMMY. I don't want it.

ELLEN. We've got to hurry, Joe. [*Takes the bottle from* JOE *and puts it on sofa up Center.*] Have you got the tickets?

JOE. Yeh, I've got them. [*Down Left to radio.*] Say, what number is the game on?

ELLEN. It's around 1210 on the dial. [*As* JOE *turns on radio and fiddles with dial—to* TOMMY.] Sure you won't go to the game?

TOMMY. Oh, no— [*With shy politeness.*] How are you?

[*DANCE MUSIC is heard on the radio.* JOE *keeps fiddling with dials trying to find the right station.*]

ELLEN. Me? I'm fine.

[*BAND MUSIC is heard on the radio.*]

TOMMY. That's good.

JOE. [*After listening to music.*] Well, it hasn't started yet—just music. Let's go. [*Gets* ELLEN'S *coat from hook.*] This yours?

[*WARN Curtain.*]

ELLEN. [*As he helps her into coat.*] Yes.

JOE. Well, is it warm enough?

ELLEN. Yes. Oh, it's very warm.

TOMMY. No, it isn't.

CLEOTA. [*Enters with thermos. Gives it to* TOMMY *at Center.*] Here's your thermos bottle, Mr. Turner.

TOMMY. Thank you. [*Takes it.*]

[CLEOTA *exits up right.*]

ELLEN. It's a very warm day, anyway, and we'll have the laprobe from the car.

TOMMY. Ellen. [*She crosses to him eagerly.*] You forgot your thermos bottle— You'd better make a note of this, Joe. It gets cold in Stadiums late in the afternoon. Ellen gets chilly sometimes, so she likes hot coffee.

[JOE *nods, goes to the Left door and opens it.* ELLEN, *who has been staring at* TOMMY, *suddenly throws the thermos bottle on the floor, then rushes out, passing* JOE. JOE *looks after her, then comes back to face* TOMMY *threateningly.*]

JOE. Did you slap her?

TOMMY. No, I kicked her.

JOE. Well, you must have done something!

[*The radio, which has been playing band music "OHIO STATE—JELLABALAD" changes to an* AN-NOUNCER'S VOICE.]

JOE. [*Picks thermos bottle up from floor, puts it on*	ANNOUNCER'S VOICE. [*Over BAND.*] Well, here

down Left table, listens to radio for a moment.] Here I get her all calmed down and you make her cry again. I see now what kind of a life she has here. I'm going to take her away from this and keep her away!

TOMMY. [*Shouting.*] All right! Why don't you get started?

we are on Midwestern field on a mighty fine afternoon for a football game. [*Voice quieter.*] It looks like the Big Day of the year, folks. Neither one of these great teams has lost a game. The Michigan squad is out on the field, warming up. They look even bigger than last year.—

JOE. [*Topping him.*] Because I've got a few more things to say to you. First! [*As he takes a breath, the* ANNOUNCER'S VOICE *comes through clearly.*]

ANNOUNCER'S VOICE. Here comes the Scarlet Stampede now! [*There is a roar of CHEERING and the Band's MUSIC swells.*]

JOE. [*Turns to radio, then in an agonized voice to* TOMMY.] My God, they're coming out on the field! We'll miss the kick-off! [*Turns and dashes out the Left door.*]

[TOMMY *stands looking after them as*

THE CURTAIN FALLS

ACT TWO

Scene II

The Turner living room, two hours later. It is growing dark outside.

TOMMY *on settee down Right and* MICHAEL *in chair Right Center, wide apart, facing the audience, so that they have to turn their heads to see each other. Each has a glass in his hand, and they are sprawled in their seats, silent, brooding. The room shows indications of quite a bout: a bottle here, a few magazines flung there, a cushion on the floor.* TOMMY *gets the Scotch bottle, pours a little into* MICHAEL'S *glass, emptying the bottle. He starts to pour some into his own glass, finds the bottle empty so pours some from* MICHAEL'S *glass into his own. Throws the bottle into waste-basket. There is a pause.*

MICHAEL. He is probably still running with that ball—

TOMMY. [*Pause.*] Quiet—quiet!— What time is it?

MICHAEL. [*Looks at wrist-watch, has trouble seeing it.*] It's getting dark.

TOMMY. [*Pause.*] Do you know the first law of human nature?

MICHAEL. Yes. Self-propagation.

TOMMY. Not any more. That's gone with last year's nightingale.

MICHAEL. Gone with last year's rose.

TOMMY. [*Slight pause.*] Yes— Defense of the home— against prowlers and predatory—prowlers— Do you know what the tiger does when the sanctity of his home is jeopardized?

MICHAEL. I know. You told me. He talks it over with the other man, quietly and calmly.

TOMMY. He does not. I'm ashamed of you.

MICHAEL. I think we must have another drink—possibly.

TOMMY. All right. Hey! *Hey!* [*He is pleased with this shouting.*] That's the way to talk to 'em. [*He puts back his head and yells.*] *HEYYY!!*

[CLEOTA *enters: she turns on the LIGHTS up Right.*]

[LIGHT cue # 1. First pipe up, start X-ray down.]

CLEOTA. [*Hurrying down to* TOMMY, *worried.*] Mistah Turner, what is it?

TOMMY. What do you want?—Oh, we should like to have something more to drink.

CLEOTA. [*Disgusted.*] Dey ain' no more to drink. I'll make you all some black coffee. [*Exits up Right.*]

TOMMY. [*Pause.*] What'd she say?

MICHAEL. Nothing.

TOMMY. Where was I?

MICHAEL. Let's see—you were talking about tigers.

TOMMY. Oh, yes. But let us take the wolf. What does

he do? I mean, when they come for his mate. He tears 'em to pieces. [*Illustrates.*]

MICHAEL. But we are civilized men. Aren't we?

TOMMY. And so does the leopard, and the lion, and the hawk. They tear 'em to pieces. Without a word.

MICHAEL. You had it figured out the other way around a while ago. You said we should give up our women. [TOMMY *stands, falters.*] It's better sitting down. [TOMMY *sits.*]

TOMMY. Let us say that the tiger wakes up one morning and finds that the wolf has come down on the fold. What does he—? Before I tell you what he does, I will tell you what he does not do.

MICHAEL. Yes, sir.

TOMMY. He does not expose everyone to a humiliating intellectual analysis. He comes out of his corner like this— [*Assumes awkward fighting pose, fists up—rises —sits quickly.*] The bull elephant in him is aroused.

MICHAEL. [*Holds up forefinger.*] Can't you stick to one animal?

TOMMY. No, that's my point. All animals are the same, including the human being. We are male animals, too.

MICHAEL. [*Stares at him, bewildered.*] You said—

TOMMY. [*With emotion.*] Even the penguin. He stands for no monkey-business where his mate is concerned. Swans have been known to drown Scotties who threatened their nests.

MICHAEL. [*After some thought.*] I don't think so.

TOMMY. There it is, in us always, though it may be asleep. The male animal. The mate. When you are married long enough, you become a mate— Think of the sea lion for a minute.

MICHAEL. All right.

TOMMY. His mate is lying there in a corner of the cave on a bed of tender boughs or something. [*Turns to* MICHAEL *for confirmation.*] Is that all right, "tender boughs"?

MICHAEL. Yeah!

TOMMY. [*Imitating fish swimming with hand gestures.*] Now, who comes swimming quietly in through the early morning mist, sleek and powerful, dancing and whirling and throwing kisses?

MICHAEL. Joe Ferguson.
                    [LIGHT cue # 2. Balcony lights full.]

TOMMY. And what do I do?

MICHAEL. You say, "Hello."

TOMMY. The sea lion knows better. He snarls. He gores. He roars with his antlers. He knows that love is a thing you do something about. He knows it is a thing that words can kill. You do something. You don't just sit there. [MICHAEL *rises.*] I don't mean you. [MICHAEL *sits.*] A woman likes a man who does something. All the male animals fight for the female, from the land crab to the bird of paradise. They don't just sit and talk. [MICHAEL *is almost asleep.*] They act. [*He has run-down, now stops, almost asleep. His head jerks and wakens him. He removes glasses and blinks owlishly around.*] I hope I have made all this clear to you. Are there any questions?

MICHAEL. [*Rousing.*] No, sir.

[ELLEN *and* JOE *enter up Left.* ELLEN *goes down Center, sees the disordered room, bottles on the floor,* TOMMY'S *and* MICHAEL'S *condition.* MICHAEL *and* TOMMY *rise.*]

ELLEN. Tommy! What in the world have you been doing?

[MICHAEL *holds out glass to illustrate.*]

TOMMY. Drinking.

ELLEN. What for?

TOMMY. [*Crossing to* ELLEN.] I was celebrating. Ellen, I have found myself. [*Sways for a second. Surveys* JOE.] I know now what I have to do.

ELLEN. Yes, I know. We've been through all that.

TOMMY. I think perhaps you had better go away for a little while. [*Waves toward upstairs.*]

ELLEN. I'm going. I'll be down in a minute, Joe. [*She slams upstairs.*]

JOE. Boy, wasn't that some football game? I'm running Wally Myers for President.

TOMMY. [*Beckoning to* MICHAEL, *who follows him to settee down Left.*] Come on. [*He and* MICHAEL *begin moving furniture to the sides of the room. Move settee Left to against Left wall.*]

JOE. [*Crosses up Right end of sofa. Watches, slightly puzzled, making talk.*] Yes, sir, some game, wasn't it?

What did you think of Michigan going into the lead like that? If Wally hadn't snared that pass—

MICHAEL. We didn't listen to the game. [*Moving coffee table to Left wall.*]

JOE. You didn't listen to the game? [*Crosses slowly to Left end of sofa.*]

MICHAEL. No, we turned it off. [*Gesture of turning off radio.*]

TOMMY. [*Crossing to chair Right Center.* MICHAEL *follows.*] The game didn't last all this time. Where have you been?

JOE. Well, we stopped in at President Cartwright's house.

TOMMY. [*They swing Right Center chair, moving it upstage a little.*] What for?

JOE. 'Cause Ellen and I were making one last effort to get you out of this mess.

TOMMY. Ellen and you. [TOMMY *and* MICHAEL *get down Right end table,* MICHAEL *on Left end,* TOMMY *Right end.*] You would know exactly what to do, wou'nt you?

JOE. You guys are pie-eyed!

TOMMY. Did you hear that? [As MICHAEL *swings his end of table all the way around up Right,* TOMMY *looks for him—then finds him upstage. They put end table down.*]

MICHAEL. Yes.

JOE. What's the idea of moving all the furniture around like this?

TOMMY. [*Crossing Center.*] I don't want you to break anything when you fall.

[MICHAEL *picks up seltzer bottles down Right Center and puts them on end table Right.*]

JOE. I'm not going to fall.

TOMMY. Yes, you are. [*Crosses to down Right table and puts down glasses; crosses Left to* JOE, *rolling up his sleeves.*] I am going to knock you cold.

[MICHAEL *sits Left arm down Right settee—faces Left.*]

JOE. [*Kindly.*] Now, Tommy—let's sit down and talk this over.

TOMMY. [*Turning to* MICHAEL.] "Talk," he says, to a man of action. [*Crossing to* MICHAEL.] "Sit down," he says, [*Crossing back to* JOE.] to a tigress and her cubs!

JOE. How in the—? How did you guys get so cock-eyed? [*Crossing to stairs.*] I wish Ellen'd hurry up. [*Crossing to up Right door.*] Cleota!

TOMMY. [*At up Left Center.*] Don't call for help. I could take Cleota and you in the same ring!

JOE. [*Crossing to* TOMMY.] Well, what's this all about?

TOMMY. You crept into this house to take Ellen away, didn't you? You thought it was the house of a professor who would talk and talk and talk—

JOE. And so you have! [*Crossing below* TOMMY *to Left Center, turns back.*] I came here to see a football game—

MICHAEL. That's a lie.

JOE. Why don't you go home?

MICHAEL. 'Cause I want to watch.

JOE. Well, there isn't going to be anything to watch.

TOMMY. [*Assuming fighter's pose.*] Come on, put up your fists.

[MICHAEL *rises, crosses to stand behind* TOMMY.]

JOE. Get away from me, Tommy. [*Pushes* TOMMY'S *arm which pivots* TOMMY *around so he faces* MICHAEL.] I'd break you in two, and I don't want to do that.

TOMMY. [*At first to* MICHAEL, *then realizing he is facing the wrong way he turns to* JOE.] Why don't you want to do that?

JOE. 'Cause how would it look if I came here and took Ellen and knocked you down on the way out?

MICHAEL. Maybe he's right. That's a point of honor, Mr. Turner.

TOMMY. Is it?

MICHAEL. But we could fight him about something else.

TOMMY. About what?

MICHAEL. He doesn't want you to read that letter.

TOMMY. [*To* MICHAEL.] That has nothing to do with this [*Realizes it has.*]—oh, yes! [MICHAEL *crosses above* TOMMY *and* JOE *to Left until he is in back of* JOE *and facing* TOMMY *who is Right Center.*] Going to President Cartwright's house. Trying to make me lose my job

JOE. Why would I?

TOMMY. So you could get Ellen.

JOE. Now, Tommy, listen—

TOMMY. Oh, yes! Now I see I'm going to have to knock you further than I had previously decided upon. Come out in the back yard. [*Pulls* JOE *who breaks away from* TOMMY.]

[MICHAEL *pushes* JOE.]

JOE. [*Turns and strides back to* MICHAEL.] Don't push me!

TOMMY. *HEY!!* [*He lunges at* JOE *with a badly aimed "haymaker."*]

JOE. [*Ducks and catches* TOMMY *to keep him from falling.*] Now look, if you do ever get in a fight, Tommy, don't lead with your right. It leaves you wide open.

TOMMY. Oh, does it?

ELLEN. [*Enters from stairs with suitcase, which she drops when she sees odd positions of belligerents.*] Tommy! What's happened? What are you doing now?

TOMMY. Fighting.

[*The music of the BAND is heard in the distance. Through the following scene it grows louder to* ELLEN'S *exit, then dies away as the BAND goes around the corner and comes up again to medium for the end of the Scene.*]

ELLEN. Fighting! What about? [*As she comes into room.*]

MICHAEL. [*Crosses Center.*] Penguins.

ELLEN. What!

JOE. [*Down Left Center. Trying to explain.*] Oh, it was all mixed up—about a lot of tigers and a cub. Tommy doesn't care what you and I are trying to do! He wants us to stay out of it!

ELLEN. [*To* TOMMY.] Oh, I see. That's what you were fighting about.

TOMMY. It wasn't about you.—Point of honor.
[*BAND grows louder.*]

ELLEN. Oh yes, I see. You don't want me mixed up with anything. All right. You can pull the house down on top of you with your birds and letters and whiskey. Just let me get out of—what is all that racket?

JOE. [*Opens the door Left a crack—then closes it and crosses down Center.*] Oh, they're having a victory parade and they want me to ride in that carriage with Wally Myers and the band. [*Crosses down Right.*]

TOMMY. [*Following* JOE.] You attract bands like flies, don't you!
[*BAND softer.*]

ELLEN. [*As she starts for Left door.*] Goodbye, Tommy! I'll be out in the car, Joe. Bring my bag, please! [*She slams out.*]

[*The* MEN *look after her.* JOE *goes up to stair landing and gets bag and crosses to* TOMMY *who sits down Right.*]

JOE. You're getting me in deeper and deeper. I should'a taken a poke at you when I had the chance!

TOMMY. [*Rising. Mad.*] Fine! Come out in the back yard! [*Walks to door down Right and opens it.*]

[MICHAEL *crosses to stand behind* JOE.]

JOE. I'm not coming out in the back yard! [MICHAEL *pushes him. Very mad, he turns on* MICHAEL.] "Don't push me!" I said, I don't like to be pushed!

TOMMY. [*Turns* JOE *around facing him.*] You said, "Don't lead with your right." [*He hits* JOE *on the nose with his left fist.*]

JOE. [*Pinching bridge of nose and dropping suitcase on settee.*] Ow-w-w! Now you've started my sinus trouble! All right, if you want a fight, you've got a fight! [*He pushes* TOMMY *outside.*]

MICHAEL. [*Pulls a chair up in front of the door and sits watching the fight offstage. He applauds its progress of blows.*] Hit him! Hit him! [*Quotes softly.*]
>"And all the summer afternoon
>They hunted us and slew!
>But tomorrow—by the living God!"

Don't forget to lead with your right, Mr. Turner!—
[*WARN Curtain.*]

That's right! Right in the eye!
[CLEOTA *enters to dining room door.* WALLY *and* PATRICIA *come in up Left laughing—see what's happening.*]

PATRICIA. Michael!! [*Rushes over down Right.*]

WALLY. What's going on here? [*Runs downstage.*]

CLEOTA. [*Up stage of down Right settee.*] Godamighty!

PATRICIA. Oh—Michael, stop them! Wally, stop them!

MICHAEL. [*Spreading arms wide across door.*] No, don't stop them! Let Mr. Turner alone and he'll tear him to pieces!

[*CRASH outside.*]

WALLY. Get away from that door! [*He hurls* MICHAEL *aside, tipping him over, goes out down Right.*]

PATRICIA. [*Runs and kneels beside* MICHAEL.] Michael! Michael!

[CLEOTA *grabs chair in which* MICHAEL *has been sitting and moves it upstage out of doorway.*]

ELLEN. [*Re-enters Left door, calling.*] Joe, are you coming? [*She sees* MICHAEL *and* PATRICIA, *and looks around the room for* TOMMY *and* JOE.]

MICHAEL. [*Sitting on the floor with* PATRICIA'S *arm around him, continues to quote poetry dramatically, declaiming toward the open door Right. With rapid fervor.*]
        "And many-a broken heart is here,"

ELLEN. What is it?

MICHAEL.
        "And many-a broken head,
          But tomorrow—by the living God!—
        We'll try the game again!"
        [*He tries to rise but collapses.*]

[JOE *and* WALLY *enter down Right carrying the unconscious* TOMMY. *They carry him to sofa up Center.*]

PATRICIA. [*Drops* MICHAEL *in disgust.*] Oh, Michael!

ELLEN. [*Screaming as she sees* TOMMY *being carried in, out cold.*] Tommy!!

> [*The PHONE rings insistently.*]

CLEOTA. [*Goes to the phone, picks up the receiver and in her usual way says.*] Professah Turner's res-i-dence!

THE CURTAIN FALLS SWIFTLY

ACT THREE

SCENE: *The Turner living room. Same as Acts One and Two.*

About noon, Monday.

The room is neat and orderly, but the flowers and other signs of festivity have been removed.

The stage is empty, but the PHONE bell is ringing. A moment later, the DOORBELL also begins to sound insistently. CLEOTA *enters from the dining room, wiping her hands on her apron, scuttles for an instant between the bells, picks up phone.*

CLEOTA. [*Into phone.*] Stop ringin' dis thing both at once—Who?—Ah cain' heah you foh de ringin'. Hol' on— [*Putting down the receiver, she hurries to the Left door and opens it cautiously, bracing herself to prevent a forced entrance. She speaks through the crack of the door.*] Ah tol' you stop ringin' eve'ything. Ah'm heah, ain' I?

REPORTER'S VOICE. [*Off.*] I'd like to see Mr. Turner.

CLEOTA. Is you a newspapah?

REPORTER'S VOICE. [*Enters, pushing her back.*] Yeh, I'm from the *Daily Journal*.

CLEOTA. [*Interrupting.*] He cain' see nobody—he's sick.

REPORTER. I know—but will he be up today? Is he going to his class?

CLEOTA. He ain' goin' nowheah. His haid huhts him. He's sick. Go 'way. [*Starts to push him out. He resists, so she shoves him away out with a* "Go way!" *She forces the door shut, bolts it, returns to the telephone.*] Professah Turner's res-i-dence— *Daily* what?—You jus' *was* heah— No, Professah Turner ain' talkin' to nobody. He's sick in bed with his haid— No, he ain' goin' an' you ain' comin'. He ain't not talkin' 'cause he don' wanta talk. He jus' ain' talkin' cause he cain' talk. Goodbye. [*The bolted Left door is rattled from outside, then the DOORBELL begins to ring insistently.* CLEOTA *looks at the door angrily and starts for it. Looks back at the phone and mutters.*] What's the matter with dis house? Will you please stop ringin' dat bell? [*As she opens door— sees* PATRICIA *and laughs, embarrassed.*] Oh! It's YOU!

PATRICIA. [*Entering.*] What's the matter? [*Puts books and purse on coffee-table down Left.*]

CLEOTA. I thought it was that newspapah again. He just left.

PATRICIA. He didn't go—he's outside picketing. [*Takes off coat—hangs it up Left.*] Where's my sister, Cleota?

CLEOTA. [*Has crossed Right, turns back to* PATRICIA.] Upstairs. Miss Patricia, Ah wish Ah knew bettah what's goin' on heah.

PATRICIA. [*Coming down.*] Never mind.

CLEOTA. Mr. Michael jus' left.

PATRICIA. [*Crosses Right to* CLEOTA.] Oh. Well, if Mr. Michael Barnes comes here again, *don't let him in!*

CLEOTA. No, ma'am. [*Exits up Right.*]

[ELLEN *comes from upstairs; she looks depressed.*]

PATRICIA. Hello, Ellen! How's Tommy? Is he still asleep?

ELLEN. Yes, but he tosses around and mutters. The doctor says he can get up this afternoon.

PATRICIA. No concussion, then?

ELLEN. Yes, a little.

PATRICIA. [*Crossing down Right, sits settee.*] I guess when anybody's as crazy as Tommy or Michael, a little concussion doesn't make any difference.

ELLEN. Did you get the butter?

PATRICIA. Oh, Lord, no—I'll go back. [*Jumps up. Starts Left.*]

ELLEN. Never mind. I need a little air. [*Crosses Left to clothes hooks.*]

PATRICIA. [*From Right Center.*] How's *your* head?

ELLEN. [*Getting coat.*] Oh, all right.

PATRICIA. Is it? [*Sits sofa Right.*] Say, what is this second springtime you're all going through, anyway?

ELLEN. [*Putting on coat.*] Tommy won't let me in on what he's really thinking about. He thinks I'm not smart enough to understand it—that's what it comes down to.

PATRICIA. Oh, a mental problem! I haven't been exactly listening at key-holes, but isn't there a Joe Something-or-other mixed up in this?

ELLEN. Oh, there's more to it than a fight about Joe.

PATRICIA. Pretty good one round here Saturday about Joe. You know Tommy was fighting for you in his mid-Victorian way, don't you?

ELLEN. Oh, but he was drunk. When he's sober he despises me. [*Crossing to Center.*] He thinks I'm a dimwit.

PATRICIA. But he wouldn't want you any other way than you are.

ELLEN. Thanks.

PATRICIA. [*Laughing.*] I mean you're smart enough for Tommy and you know it, and he knows it.

ELLEN. I'm all mixed up. [*Crossing Left up Left Center.*] I want to go away some place where I can think.

PATRICIA. Look, this is a new century. You're not Diana of the Crossways or somebody.

ELLEN. [*Turns back to PATRICIA.*] Well, what do you want me to do—stay here when he doesn't want me?

PATRICIA. No, but if you're going away, go away with Joe. Tommy's certainly been throwing you at him. Why don't you take him up on it? See what happens.

ELLEN. [*Crossing in a few steps.*] Is this advice to the lovelorn? Do you think he would come running after me?

PATRICIA. Well, you've got to quit moping around and do something. I thought we Stanley women were supposed to have some resources. [*Rises; crossing Left to ELLEN.*] Look, your great-grandmother chased her man all the way to Nebraska in a covered wagon.

ELLEN. Well, I'm not going to chase anybody anywhere!

I'm going to talk this over with Tommy, fairly and squarely, face to face. [*Crosses up Left to door and opens it.*]

PATRICIA. "Fairly and squarely!" How did your generation ever get through the 1920's?

ELLEN. [*Sadly.*] We didn't. [*She exits.*]

[PATRICIA *sits on sofa up Center; sighs.*]

TOMMY. [*Comes slowly down stairs. He wears terrycloth bathrobe, and has a wet turkish towel twisted about his head.*] Hello, Pat!

PATRICIA. [*Rises. Worried.*] Tommy—you shouldn't be up!

TOMMY. I'm all right. What day is this?

PATRICIA. Monday.

TOMMY. [*Calls off up Right.*] Cleota—Cleota! [*To* PATRICIA.] Can I take this thing off? [*Moves down.*]

PATRICIA. You're not supposed to. You ought to lie down.

TOMMY. [*Sits chair Right Center.*] I'll just lean back. [*Does so. Winces.*] No—I guess I won't.

CLEOTA. [*Appears in Right door. Sees* TOMMY.] Mistah Turner—is you up?

TOMMY. Yes, I'm up. Cleota, don't let anyone in this house except Mr. Michael Barnes.

[PATRICIA *shakes her head violently "No" to* CLEOTA *from above* TOMMY.]

CLEOTA. Yessuh—Ah do de best Ah can. [*Exits up Right.*]

TOMMY. Where's Ellen?

PATRICIA. [*Saunters down Right to settee. Sits.*] She went out to [*Teasing.*] to get the transfer man—for her trunk.

TOMMY. She's going away?

PATRICIA. Oh, no. She just likes to call on transfer men. Didn't you know that?

TOMMY. I can't stand irony so early in the day, Patricia.

PATRICIA. You're all right now, you see. She wouldn't go before. I don't know why.

TOMMY. You ought to know why. Your sister wouldn't walk out on anybody when he's down—even when he's down with delirium tremens.

PATRICIA. You didn't have D.T.'s. You had concussion.

TOMMY. Seemed more like D.T.'s.

PATRICIA. You don't know very much about my little sister, do you?

TOMMY. I know a lot more than I did last Friday. [*Rises. Crossing up to sofa Center.*] I think I will lie down.

PATRICIA. Why do you have to make everything as hard as you can? [TOMMY *winces with pain. She rises. Crossing to him.*] Do you want another cold towel?

TOMMY. [*Patting her arm.*] No, thanks. [*PHONE rings. Lies back on sofa.*] Oh, those bells!!

PATRICIA. [*Crosses. Answering phone.*] Yes?—Who? No, Michael Barnes isn't here.

TOMMY. He was here and he's coming back.

PATRICIA. This is Patricia Stanley— Yes— Yes— I'll be very glad to tell him to call you—if I see him. Goodbye! [*Slams receiver down.*] That was Hot Cha-cha Gardner.

TOMMY. Oh-oh! Why did she call here?

PATRICIA. [*Turns up Right Center.*] She said they told her Michael was on his way here, but obviously she just called for my benefit— So that's where he went Saturday night! [*Turning to* TOMMY.] You had that Hot—that Miss Gardner in some of your classes; do you remember her?

TOMMY. [*Reflectively. Sitting up.*] I don't know. What does she look like?

PATRICIA. Well, she—doesn't wear any— [*Gestures.*]

TOMMY. [*Lying back.*] I only had her in Wordsworth.

PATRICIA. [*Turns Right.*] Calling up here! [*There is a KNOCK at the door up Left;* PATRICIA *smiles grimly. She goes up and opens the door.* MICHAEL *steps in; he is taken aback at seeing* PATRICIA.] Good-morning, Michael! Come in.

TOMMY. [*Sits up. Peering over his shoulder.*] Yes, come in, Michael. [*Pantomimes "telephone" for* MICHAEL'S *benefit.*]

MICHAEL. [*Comes down a little nervously and stands near* TOMMY.] I got the car for you—[PATRICIA *crosses to below settee down Right*]—Feel better now that you're up? [*Doesn't get the pantomime.*]

TOMMY. [*Pantomiming.*] Yes, much better. How do you feel?

MICHAEL. I feel all right.

TOMMY. That's good. [*Mimics* PATRICIA'S *gesture.*]

[MICHAEL *doesn't get it. Looks inside his coat to see what's wrong.* PATRICIA *turns and catches pantomime.*]

PATRICIA. [*Crosses up Left; gets coat, then crosses to down Left table for purse.*] If you'll excuse me—

MICHAEL. [*Coming down Left to her.*] Oh, Pat, wait! —I—could I talk to you for a minute? Couldn't we go outside there and—

PATRICIA. [*Proud and angry.*] No. we couldn't go outside there. Is it anything you're ashamed to say in front of Tommy?

MICHAEL. [*Stiffening.*] No. No, I'm not. Only— Well, I don't want to get off on the wrong foot again. I'm sorry I got so mad Saturday. I said things and did things that—

PATRICIA. You certainly did.

MICHAEL. [*Shouting.*] Well, I'm sorry, and— [*Then, reasonably.*] Oh, Pat, you ought to be able to see this my way. We just lost our tempers and—well—Mr. Turner and I are in a jam. I think you ought to—well— make an effort to understand what we're trying to do and stand by us—that is, if you care anything about me at all.

PATRICIA. [*With false sweetness.*] Oh, I certainly do. I've been standing by—taking messages for you—phone calls. I'm so glad we had this nice talk. [*Shakes his hand.*] And before you go, be sure to call [*Dropping her sweetness, she yells:*] Maple 4307. [PATRICIA *flounces out door up Left.*]

MICHAEL. [*Looking after her.*] Maple 430— [*Crossing up to* TOMMY.] Did The Cha-cha call here?

TOMMY. That's what I was trying to tell you. Patricia answered the phone. The—Chow-chow—snapped right in her face.

MICHAEL. And I didn't even *do* anything. [*Sits on sofa.*] I hope. [*Looks up miserably.*]

TOMMY. Michael, you're making me nervous. [*Moves further Right on sofa.*]

MICHAEL. Will you be able to go to the faculty meeting tonight?

TOMMY. I'll be there.

MICHAEL. They'll be out to get you—I know this is all my fault, Mr. Turner.

TOMMY. Yes, you're certainly the man that lighted the match.

MICHAEL. I just came from the President's office; he flayed me alive.

TOMMY. Are you kicked out?

MICHAEL. Suspended.

TOMMY. Michael, tell me— Are you really a Communist?

MICHAEL. Me?—No—I only know one guy who is. I'm
—well, I guess I'm an unconfused liberal. I think I'll go
to Stringfellow Barr's school in Annapolis and read the
classics.

TOMMY. I wonder where I'll go?

[ELLEN *enters Left with parcel.*]

ELLEN. Good morning, Michael.

MICHAEL. [*Rises.*] Hello, Mrs. Turner!

ELLEN. [*Sees* TOMMY.] Good morning, Tommy—
[*Crossing to up Right door. Calls.*] Cleota—

TOMMY. Good morning.

[CLEOTA *enters up Right.*]

ELLEN. Here's the butter, Cleota. Will you make Mr.
Turner a cup of tea? [*Turns back to him.*] Would you
like a hard-boiled egg?

TOMMY. No, thanks. Nothing hard. My teeth hurt.

[CLEOTA *exits.*]

ELLEN. [*Crossing up Left takes off coat, hangs it up.*]
Are you waiting for Patricia, Michael?

MICHAEL. I saw her. I'm leaving town, Mrs. Turner.

ELLEN. I'm awfully sorry, Michael.

WALLY'S VOICE. [*Off Right.*] Pat! Oh, Pat!

ELLEN. Come in, Wally. [*Crossing downstage.* WALLY
comes in down Right.] Patricia's gone out somewhere.

WALLY. Oh, I see. [*To* MICHAEL.] You waiting for her?

MICHAEL. [*Crossing down Right to him.*] That's none of your business. Why?

WALLY. [*Crossing in to* MICHAEL. *Lowers his voice.*] I know what you did Saturday night, that's why. [*Crossing below* MICHAEL *to* ELLEN.] Well, thanks, Mrs. Turner. I just cut across the back way. I'll walk on down to the house. [*Starts out down Right.*]

MICHAEL. [*Stops him.*] I think I'll walk along. I want to talk to you.

WALLY. You don't have to. [*Pushes* MICHAEL.]

MICHAEL. If I didn't have to, I wouldn't do it. I'm no masochist. [*Starts out down Right and punches* WALLY *in stomach.*]

WALLY. [*Stares after him blankly, then follows, furious.*] You don't have to use words like that in front of ladies.

MICHAEL. I'll be back in time to drive you to class, Mr. Turner. [*Turns and* WALLY *bumps into him.* MICHAEL *pushes* WALLY *out down Right.*]

TOMMY. Thanks.

ELLEN. [*Takes tea from* CLEOTA *who has entered up Right with cup on tray.*] Here's your tea.

[CLEOTA GOES OUT.]

TOMMY. Thanks.

ELLEN. [*With some constraint.*] How do you feel?

TOMMY. Very strange.

ELLEN. Is everything clear to you now?

TOMMY. [*Stirs tea.*] Clear in the center. It's kind of fuzzy around the edges.

ELLEN. [*Crossing down Right; sits on settee.*] I hope it's clear enough to give me a chance to say something without your going off on one of your literary tangents.

TOMMY. I don't do that.

ELLEN. I know you think I'm not very bright or something, [TOMMY *tries to demur, but she continues.*] but you must realize that you got me all mixed up Friday and that you were even less helpful Saturday.

TOMMY. That wasn't me, Saturday. That was a drunken sea lion.

ELLEN. I rather liked you as a sea lion.

TOMMY. Yes, I must have been very funny. Did you ever read Hodgson's poem, "The Bull"?

ELLEN. [*Turns to him.*] Oh, Tommy!

TOMMY. It's the story of the defeated male. There is no defeat that can be quite so complete.

ELLEN. You wouldn't admit that this defeat was on account of— No, it has to be something out of a book.

TOMMY. When the bull's head is in the dust, life goes on and leaves him there; it's a psychological fact. The poets understand these things.

ELLEN. And all the cows react the same way? As if they were reading instructions from a blackboard? Oh, Tommy, listen to me— [*Rises. Crosses to* TOMMY.]
[*DOORBELL rings.*]

TOMMY. The point is, I don't want any pity.

CLEOTA. [*Entering from dining room.*] Miz Turner! Miz Turner! It's dat prize-fightah. I seen him from de windah.

[ELLEN *admits* JOE *Left, who comes in without his old bounce; he is worried and restless.* CLEOTA *stands in up Right doorway, hanging onto every word.*]

ELLEN. Hello, Joe!

JOE. Hello. [*Awkwardly to* TOMMY.] Hello.

TOMMY. Hello!

JOE. I'm sorry, Tommy. I didn't hit you hard. You slipped and hit your head on a bench.

[ELLEN *sits Right arm down Left settee.*]

TOMMY. Yeh, I know. What's the matter with your hand?

JOE. You kinda bit me. Ed's out in the car. We just chased a reporter away hanging around out there.

ELLEN. Well, don't let any reporters in, Cleota.

TOMMY. And don't let Keller in.

[CLEOTA *nods and exits up Right.*]

JOE. [*Indicating wet towel.*] Do you have to keep that thing on?

TOMMY. No, I just do it because I like it. [*Throws down towel.*]

JOE. Could I have a little slug of something? I—

ELLEN. [*Rises.*] Certainly! Scotch?

JOE. Yeh, fine. [ELLEN *exits up Right.* JOE *crosses down Right. There is a pause.* JOE *still wonders about the vanished cup.*] I got the galloping jumps. I can use a little drink. Haven't slept for two nights.

TOMMY. Worrying about something?

JOE. [*Turns to* TOMMY.] Yeh, worrying about something— And my cold's worse.

TOMMY. Want some Kleenex?

JOE. [*Irritated.*] No, I don't want some Kleenex. [*Crossing Left.*] Darn reporters been bothering me, too.

TOMMY. What do they want with you?

JOE. Oh, they wanted me to pick an all-American team.

TOMMY. [*Incredulously—almost.*] Did you?

JOE. Yeh. Kinda took my mind off things.

TOMMY. [*Sarcastically.*] Who'd you pick for right guard?

JOE. Shulig—Kansas State Teachers'. [*Crossing to* TOMMY.] Look, Tommy, where the hell do we all stand now? [TOMMY *picks up towel, presses it to his head again.*] Does that kinda throb?

TOMMY. No.

JOE. Well, I wanta know where we all stand.

TOMMY. Oh, let it alone, Joe. It'll work out. You and I can handle this. I don't want Ellen worried about details now. She's got enough trouble with me—sitting around the house looking like a hot-oil shampoo—

ELLEN. [*Enters with bottle of Scotch. She pours a drink of straight Scotch at table up Right.*] There's been more drinking in this house in the last two days than we've done in ten years.

[JOE *takes off coat, puts it up Left chair; crosses and sits down Left.*]

TOMMY. [*After a pause.*] Ellen, Joe picked Shulig of Kansas State Teachers' for right guard, on his All-American. Isn't that nice?

JOE. [*Reminiscently.*] It was kinda hard choosing between him and Feldkamp of Western Reserve. Both big and fast.

ELLEN. [*Crossing with drink.*] Here you are, dear— [*She is coolly oblivious of* TOMMY'S *hand which he puts out for drink; goes on to* JOE, *who doesn't realize she means him.*] Dear. [*He looks up at her with a start— looks at* TOMMY—*takes drink.*]

TOMMY. I don't want any.

JOE. Say, have you got a Pennsylvania time-table around?

ELLEN. [*Crossing up, gets* TOMMY'S *cup and saucer.*] Where are you going, Joe?

JOE. Well, I've got to be in Washington tomorrow.

ELLEN. That's going to rush me.

JOE. What do you mean?

ELLEN. [*Crossing above settee down Left.*] Well, Joe, I thought you and I might start out late this afternoon and go as far as that little Inn at Granville tonight. Just for a start. [*Puts teacup and saucer on down Left table, sits close to* JOE.]

TOMMY. [*Rises.*] What did you say?

ELLEN. [*To* JOE.] I think it's the nicest place around here. Don't you?

JOE. I—I—eh— Could I have a little more Scotch? [*Rises; crosses up Right; gets another drink.*]

ELLEN. I don't want you to get drunk, Joe.

JOE. I'll be all right—I'll be all right. What time is it?

TOMMY. Never mind what time it is. [*Crossing to* EL-LEN.] Would you mind explaining this a little better?

ELLEN. I'll try to make it as clear as I can for both of you. I simply have to make a fresh start now, Tommy. You understand women; you must see that. I can't stay here now. You've made your plans, and now I have to make mine.

TOMMY. Yes—but not like this—not running off to Granville!

ELLEN. All right, if you're afraid of a scandal, we'll go farther away. Put Granville out of your mind, then. We'll go directly to Pittsburgh.

JOE. [*Coming down.*] Huh?

ELLEN. It's a very big town. Nobody need know **any**thing about it.

JOE. [*Coming down a step.*] About what?

ELLEN. About us. About our eloping together.

[*Both* MEN *stop cold.*]

TOMMY. Ellen!

JOE. [*Desperately crossing Center.*] But you see—I don't live in Pittsburgh. [*He makes a large circular gesture.*] I live in Sewickly. [*Gesture—small.*] And my boss lives there too. [*Starts down Right.*] And my mother. My mother's not very well. My mother—

TOMMY. Oh, you and your mother!

JOE. [*Crossing Left a little.*] Besides, it's a Presbyterian town.

ELLEN. You're not being very gallant, Joe.

TOMMY. [*Crossing to* JOE.] No. Are you trying to get out of this?

JOE. No, but I come from a long line of married people! [TOMMY *crosses below* JOE *to down Right.*] And besides, I'm not going to Pittsburgh directly. I've got to go to Washington, [*Crossing to* ELLEN.] and that's one place I couldn't take you, Ellen!

TOMMY. You'll take her any place she wants to go, but she's not going any place!

ELLEN. Oh, yes, I am!

ED. [*There is a loud KNOCK, and* ED KELLER *enters Left.*] I can't sit out in that car all day, you know.

JOE. [*Takes* ED'S *hat off, puts it on up Center table.*] Oh, I'm sorry, Ed, but—jees, I forgot all about you. [JOE *turns to* TOMMY.] I persuaded Ed to come over and talk to you before this thing gets too bad. [*Leads* ED *down Right Center to* TOMMY.]

TOMMY. It couldn't get any worse!

JOE. I mean about the trustees.

TOMMY. Let the trustees take care of themselves. We have troubles of our own. [*Sits down Right settee.*]

ED. You'll find out this is your trouble. [JOE *goes up Left, closes door. To* JOE.] Is he able to talk?

JOE. Lord, yes!

ED. [*Crossing to* TOMMY.] Well, then, listen. We just had a trustees' meeting in the President's office. Michael Barnes is out, and you're on your way out. You'll be asked to resign tonight.

ELLEN. [*Rising.*] Oh, Tommy!

JOE. Ed's trying to help him while there's still time. After tonight, it will be too late. [*Goes above settee Left.*]

TOMMY. [*Rises; crossing up Left.*] What do you care what happens tonight? You won't be here. You'll be in Granville or somewhere.

[JOE *turns away to fireplace Left.*]

ED. What're you going to be doing in Granville?

TOMMY. Please don't ask personal questions.

ELLEN. Do you mind if I stay a little while, Tommy?

TOMMY. [*Angrily.*] Why shouldn't you stay? It's your house.

ED. Sit down, Ellen. [*She sits down Left.* ED *crossing to* TOMMY *at Left Center.*] There's just one thing you can do: come out with a statement to the papers quick. Say you were sick. Say you didn't know anything about

Barnes' editorial. You think it's an outrage. You're not going to read this Vanzetti thing, and you think Barnes is getting what he deserves. That's the only thing that'll save your neck.

ELLEN. [*Rises.*] Tommy wouldn't say that about Michael, Ed, and you shouldn't ask him to.

TOMMY. Thank you. [*Crosses down Right to settee; sits.*]

ED. All right, then! That's all I had to say. [*Starts for door up Left.*] Goodbye! This is on your own head.

ELLEN. Ed! Just a minute, please. [*Crossing to* TOMMY.] I know that reading this letter must mean something to you, Tommy. Something none of us can quite understand. I wish I could. It might help me to understand a lot of other things, when I can get away where I can think.

TOMMY. Such as what?

ELLEN. Such as what is important to you. What you've been fighting for. Whether it's something you really believe in and love, or just your own selfish pride. I think you got into this just because you were mad at me. And that's ridiculous, because now you don't care what I do or say about it. You're out of that.

ED. [*Coming down Center.*] I don't see what she's talking about.

[JOE *motions him to be quiet.*]

TOMMY. All right, I'll try to explain what it means to me. Perhaps originally pride had something to do with this. And jealousy.

ELLEN. And stubbornness—

TOMMY. And—please. [*Rises.*] I am trying to say that
—now—I am not fighting about you and me at all. This
is bigger than you and me or any of us.

ELLEN. Is it?

ED. [*Ironically.*] It must be a masterpiece. That letter
must be quite a nice piece of propaganda.

TOMMY. [*Crossing Center to him.*] Why don't you read
it and find out?

ED. I don't read things like that.

TOMMY. You don't even know what you're objecting to.

JOE. [*At fireplace.*] Well, Tommy, why don't you read
the letter to us, and let us see what it is?

TOMMY. I'll be glad to read it to you, but I'll read it to
my class too. [*Crosses up Right Center to bookcase.*]

ED. [*Crossing down.*] You don't have to read it to me. I
know what kind of stuff it is.

[*The Left door bursts open, and* PATRICIA *backs in,
leaving the door open.* WALLY *is outside. They talk in
excited undertones.* TOMMY *looks through up Right
Center bookcase.* ED *removes coat, puts it on up Center
sofa.*]

PATRICIA. But I can't go with you now! I told you I've
got to wait here and see what Tommy's going to do.

WALLY. [*Off Left.*] But you're not going to the class!
You said you're not going!

PATRICIA. I'm not! I just want to know!

WALLY. [*Off.*] I'll bet you *are* going! You're waiting here for Michael to go with you!

PATRICIA. Oh, go away! [*Sees* OTHERS.] Oh—I'm sorry. [*Crosses down Right.*]

[WALLY *enters and crosses down to above settee Left.*]

ED. What's this now?

JOE. [*Grinning.*] Hey, Pat, you better think twice before you scrap with Wally here. [TOMMY *goes upstairs for book.*] He's coming in with me at Pittsburgh next year.

WALLY. [*Crossing to* JOE *Left.*] A lot she cares about Pittsburgh! I run sixty-two yards through Michigan and all she wants is to listen to Mike Barnes talk about his love life. [*Crosses down Right.*]

ED. She does?

ELLEN. [*Trying to stop him, at chair Right Center.*] Wally, how's Stalenkiwiecz?

WALLY. He's much better. [*Crossing to* PATRICIA *down Right.*] If you knew what I know about that guy Barnes—

PATRICIA. I know what you're hinting at! And what if he did? It only shows what an intense person Michael is. I know that no matter what he did, he was thinking of me.

WALLY. That's disgusting!

PATRICIA. And aren't you a little bit disgusting to mention it? I thought *men* had some loyalty! [*She goes out down Right.*]

WALLY. [*Following her out.*] Now, listen here— Do you know what he did?—I'll tell you what he did.

ED. What kind of a house is this?

[*As they go out the lower door,* DAMON, *carrying an umbrella, walks quietly in the open front door and looks around, as* TOMMY *comes downstairs with an open book in his hand.*]

TOMMY. [*Coming Center.*] All right, here it is. Now sit down—or stand up—but listen!— [JOE *sits on fireplace bench Left;* ED *sits up Center sofa.*] Oh, come in, Doctor Damon. You're just in time.

DAMON. [*Closes the front door, comes downstage.*] In time for what? [*Sees them.*] Has the Inquisition moved its headquarters?

TOMMY. I'm just going to read the Inquisition a letter from one of its victims.

ED. That's about enough of that.

DAMON. [*Crossing down Left.*] Gentlemen, gentlemen— This may not be wise, Thomas.

TOMMY. It may not be wise, but it's necessary. I think you'll have to take a stand, too, Doctor Damon.

DAMON. I hope not. [*Sits down Left settee.*]

[ELLEN *sits end of down Right settee.*]

TOMMY. So did I hope not. I didn't start out to lead a crusade. I simply mentioned one day that I meant to read to my class three letters by men whose profession was not literature, but who had something sincere to say. [*Crossing Right.*] Once I had declared that very harmless intention, the world began to shake, great institutions trembled, and football players descended upon me and my wife. I realized then that I was doing something important.

ED. [*Sarcastically.*] You make it sound mighty innocent. Reading Lincoln and General Sherman—and Vanzetti. What was the reason you gave for picking out Vanzetti?

TOMMY. [*Crosses to* ED.] Originally I chose him to show that broken English can sometimes be very moving and eloquent, but now—

ED. We wouldn't object if this was just a case of broken English—it's more than that.

TOMMY. Yes, you've made it more than that.

ED. Vanzetti was an anarchist! He was executed for murder.

TOMMY. He was accused of murder, but thousands of people believe he was executed simply because of the ideas he believed in.

ED. That's a dangerous thing to bring up.

TOMMY. [*Getting really mad.*] No, it's a dangerous thing to keep down. I'm fighting for a teacher's rights. But if you want to make it political, all right! You can't suppress ideas because you don't like them—not in this country—not yet. [*Crossing to* DAMON.] This is a university! It's our business to bring what light we can into this muddled world—to try to follow truth!

DAMON. You may be right, Thomas, but I wish you would make an effort not to—uh—uh—intone.

TOMMY. I'm not intoning—I'm yelling! Don't you see

this isn't about Vanzetti. This is about us! If I can't read this letter today, tomorrow none of us will be able to teach anything except what Mr. Keller here and the Legislature permit us to teach. Can't you see what that leads to—what it has led to in other places? We're holding the last fortress of free thought, and if we surrender to prejudice and dictation, we're cowards. [*Crossing Right.*]

ELLEN. [*From Right settee.*] Tommy, no matter how deeply you feel about this, what can you *do?* What can any one man do? Except to lose everything—

TOMMY. [*Crossing to* ELLEN.] I have very little more to lose. And I can't tell you what I hope to gain. I can't answer that. I only know that I have to do it.

[PATRICIA *appears in doorway, down Right, stops and listens.*]

DAMON. May we hear the letter—in a slightly calmer mood, perhaps?

TOMMY. Yes, sir— [*Crossing up to* ED.] This may disappoint you a little, Mr. Keller. It isn't inflammatory, so it may make you feel a little silly. At least, I hope so— [*He holds up the book, pauses.* ED *and* JOE *get set in their seats.*] Vanzetti wrote this in April, 1927, after he was sentenced to die. It has been printed in many newspapers. It appears in this book. You could destroy every printed copy of it, but it would not die out of the language, because a great many people know it by heart. [*He reads, hardly referring to the book, watching them.*] "If it had not been for these thing, I might have live out my life talking at street corners to scorning men. I might have die, unmarked, unknown, a failure. Now we are not a failure. Never in our full life could we hope to do so much work for tolerance, for Justice, for man's understanding of man, as now we do by accident. Our words—our lives—our pain—nothing! The taking of our lives—the lives of a good shoemaker and a poor fish-peddler—all! That last moment belongs to us—that agony is our triumph!" [*He closes the book. There is silence for a moment.*] Well, that's it— [*Crosses up Right; puts book up Right table.*]

[KELLER *is puzzled;* ELLEN, *who has been moved by the letter, looks up in surprise, meets* TOMMY'S *eyes, then drops hers.*]

JOE. [*Uncomfortably.*] Well, that isn't so bad! That isn't a bad letter.

[DAMON *is delighted at this reaction.*]

ED. Is that all of it?

TOMMY. Yes, that's all.

JOE. [*Rises. Crossing to* ED.] Maybe Tommy's right. I don't see that it would do so much harm.

ED. [*Slowly.*] Yes, it will. If he reads this letter to his class he'll get a lot of those kids worried about that man. Make socialists out of 'em.

JOE. [*Crosses down Left.*] It's got me worried already.

ED. [*Rises.*] No— I won't have it—— You fellows are trying to defy the authority of the trustees. You say you're going to take a stand. Well, we've *taken* a stand. I wouldn't care if that letter were by Alexander Hamilton.

TOMMY. [*Crossing to* ED.] Neither would I. The principle is exactly the same.

JOE. [*Speaking hopefully.*] Well, then, read something else. Why can't you read Hoover?

ED. Yeah.

JOE. He writes a lot of stuff—a lot of good stuff in his book.

TOMMY. Hoover can't write as well as Vanzetti.

ED. [*Winces.*] That's a terrible thing to say. You'll get in trouble saying things like that.

TOMMY. [*Crossing down Right.*] Very likely.

JOE. [*Crossing to* ED.] Ed, look—can't we compromise somehow? Seems a shame that a little thing like this should—

ELLEN. [*Rises.*] It isn't little! Joe, you have some influence around here.

TOMMY. I can fight my own battles, Ellen.

ELLEN. Can't I say anything any more—not even on your side?

ED. [*Crossing to* TOMMY; *stopped by* TOMMY's *line.*] All right, Turner, I've heard the letter and—

TOMMY. [*Answering* ELLEN.] Not out of a sense of self-sacrifice or something.

ED. What?

ELLEN. Oh, yes, you always know—

ED. [*To* JOE.] Do we always have to have women butting into this?

JOE. Ellen isn't women. She's Tommy's wife.

ELLEN. No, I'm not—

ED. [*Crossing to* TOMMY.] No, Turner, it comes to this— [*Turns to* ELLEN.] You're not what? Do you mean to stand there and tell me you two are not—

TOMMY. Will you please not ask personal questions?

ED. [*Turns to* TOMMY.] No. *We can't have that in this school!*

ELLEN. It's Joe and I who are going away together.

ED. [*To* TOMMY.] Yeh, will you let me— [*Turns to* ELLEN.] You and Joe are going to what! [*Crosses to* JOE *Left Center.*] What the—what is going on here anyway?

JOE. Now don't look at me!

ED. You can't go away with Ellen!

JOE. I didn't say—

ELLEN. [*Sits down Right settee.*] We might as well tell him now. I'm going to Pittsburgh with Joe.

ED. [*Crossing back to* ELLEN.] Why, you can't do that! Why, the newspapers would make Midwestern University look like some kind of a honky-tonk or something. This is worse than that damn letter!

[PATRICIA *crosses up; sits stair landing.*]

TOMMY. Aren't you getting off the subject? [*Crosses around Left toward* ED.]

ED. No! What kind of a woman are you?

TOMMY. [*Crossing above* ELLEN *to* ED.] You come out in the back yard! Right out in the back yard!

JOE. [*In a step.*] Be careful, Ed!

[TOMMY *crosses down Left.*]

ELLEN. No more fights please!

DAMON. [*Rises.*] I think I shall get a breath of fresh air. [*Goes to door up Left, opens it.*]

ELLEN. Well, I can't stay *here* now.

JOE. Look, Ed, you don't understand. You get things all mixed up.

ED. [*Crossing to down Left Center.*] Well, I've got this much straight—if we can keep sex out of this for a minute. I came here to say to you that if you read this letter today you're out of this university tomorrow! You take this stand and you stand alone!

DAMON. [*Crossing down to* ED.] Mr. Keller, for forty-two years I have followed a policy of appeasement. I might say I have been kicked around in this institution by one Edward K. Keller after another—

ED. There is only one Edward K. Keller.

DAMON. There has always been at least one. But there is an increasing element in the faculty which resents your attitude toward any teacher who raises his voice or so much as clears his throat. I warn you that if you persist in persecuting Thomas Turner, you will have a fight on your hands, my friend.

ED. Do you think that Bryson and Kressinger and I are afraid of a few dissatisfied book-worms who work for twenty-five hundred a year?

DAMON. [*Furious.*] These men are not malcontents! Some of them are distinguished scholars who have made this University what it is!

ED. They've made it what it is! What about me? Who's getting this new stadium? Who brought Coach Sprague here from Southern Methodist?

JOE. [*Crossing to* ED.] He means that this thing is bigger than stadiums and coaches.

ED. [*Crossing up to* JOE.] Nothing's bigger than the new stadium.

[DAMON *crosses Left to* TOMMY.]

JOE. Now we've all had a bad week-end around here, and you're not helping any.

ED. Do you think I've had a good week-end! [*Crosses Left Center.*]

[MICHAEL *and* NUTSY *enter up Left with petition.*]

MICHAEL. [*Crossing down Left.*] Come in, Nutsy.

[DAMON *crosses to down Left settee; sits.*]

ED. Now what!

MICHAEL. We're circulating petitions for Mr. Turner. Show 'em, Nutsy.

NUTSY. [*Crossing below* ED *to* JOE *at Center.*] This one's just from 14th Avenue and the Athletic house. [*Turns to* TOMMY.] We've got three hundred and fifty-seven names.

DAMON. We want no student insurrections!

JOE. Let me see that thing. [*Takes petition from* NUTSY; *crosses up Right—*NUTSY *follows.*]

ED. [*Crossing down Right Center.*] You're wasting your time with that handful of names. Turner will be out tomorrow and Barnes is on his way home now.

MICHAEL. [*Crossing to* ED.] I'm not on my way home yet, sir.

ED. [*Turns to* MICHAEL.] *Ohhh!* So you're Barnes! So you're the little puppy that called me a Fascist!

PATRICIA. [*Rises; crossing down between* ED *and* MICHAEL. *To* ED.] Well, the way you're treating everybody, I think you *are* a Fascist!

ELLEN. Patricia!

TOMMY. [*Up Left.*] Let her alone.

ELLEN. Oh, she can stand up for Michael, but I can't stand up for you! Is that it?

TOMMY. This is—ah—different.

ED. Do I have to stand here and be insulted by every sixteen-year-old child that comes into this room?

PATRICIA. I'm not sixteen, I'm nineteen!

MICHAEL. She'll soon be twenty.

ED. [*To* MICHAEL.] Why don't *you* get packing?

MICHAEL. You don't need to worry about me. I'll be far away from here by tomorrow. Come on, Nutsy!

[*Crosses up Left.* NUTSY *exits Left.*]

PATRICIA. [*Starts after him.*] If you throw him out, I'm going with him! Wait, Michael! [*Crosses to door Left.*]

ED. Are you married to this little radical?

PATRICIA. You don't have to be married to somebody **to** go away with him—do you, Ellen? [*Exits.*]

[MICHAEL *follows her out.*]

DAMON. [*Rises. Crossing up Left.*] I think I shall go home, have my Ovaltine and lie down. [*Exit Left, closing door.*]

ED. He'll need his Ovaltine. [Crosses upstage.]

JOE. [*Crossing to* ED.] Say, Ed, look! This thing has been signed by Stalenkiwiecz and Wierasocka.

ED. [*Crossing to* JOE.] What! I don't believe it. [*Takes petition, looks at it.*]

JOE. Ed, you ought to have some respect for men like Dean Damon and Stalenkiwiecz and Wierasocka.

ED. They can't do this to me! Two of the biggest men in the university signing the Red petition! You, the greatest half-back we ever had, running away with a woman! Why—they'll never ask us to the Rose Bowl now!

TOMMY. [*Crossing up Left.*] What is the Rose Bowl?

ED. [*Thrusts petition into* JOE's *hand.*] I'm getting **out** of this house! Coming Joe?

JOE. No.

ED. [*Putting on coat.*] You can't depend on anybody! I've a damn good notion to resign from the board of trustees. [*To* TOMMY.] But I'll kick you out if it's the last thing I do.

TOMMY. [*Crossing up Left.*] Just to make things even— I'll kick you out. Here's your hat. [*Opens door, gives him* JOE'S *derby from up Center table.*]

ED. We'll see! [*Puts on hat and stomps out.*]

JOE. Hey, that's my hat!

TOMMY. Well, get another one. [*Closes door.*] Well, that's that.

[*They look at each other.*]

JOE. Yeh, that's that. [*Pause. Crossing down Left.*] Well, I s'pose Ed will never speak to me again.

TOMMY. [*Takes his own coat and hat from hook, puts them on end of sofa.*] I have to go to class. I'll be late. [*Starts for stairs.*]

ELLEN. [*Appealingly. Crossing to* TOMMY.] Tommy— I—

TOMMY. I know. I know.

ELLEN. You know what?

TOMMY. I know what you're going to say—but I don't want substitutes. I don't want *loyalty*.

[ELLEN *turns away.*]

JOE. [*Down Left Center.*] What's the matter with that?

TOMMY. I just don't want Ellen standing by like a Red Cross nurse because she knows I'm in trouble.

JOE. I don't know whether you need a nurse or a psychoanalyst!

ELLEN. I think he's analyzed it very well himself. It isn't because you think I don't care, it's because you don't.

TOMMY. [*Crossing down Left to coffee table, almost bursting.*] I thought we could settle this *quietly* and *calmly.*

ELLEN. Quietly and calmly! Oh, Lord! [*Picks up large ashtray Right table—smashes it on floor.*]

TOMMY. Now, don't do that! I can throw things, too! [*Picks up cup down Left table.*]

ELLEN. [*Crossing Right Center.*] No, you can't—you haven't got enough blood in you!

[TOMMY *glares at her, puts cup down coldly—suddenly snatches it and crashes it into fireplace—reaches for saucer.*]

JOE. [*Leaps for* TOMMY—*grabs saucer from him.*] Now wait—let me handle this. I don't throw things— I just want to say that I came to this city to see a football game.

ELLEN. [*Crossing to* JOE *Left Center.*] Oh, no, you didn't! You came for me. You haven't been here for a ball-game in ten years. You wait till Brenda and you are separated, then you come for me!

JOE. Oh, hell! [*Throws saucer in fireplace then wilts as he realizes this household has affected him, too.*]

TOMMY. [*Crossing above* JOE *to between them down Left Center, desperately insisting upon his own doom.*] That's very smart, Ellen. That's very penetrating. That's all I wanted to know. [*To* JOE.] Subconsciously, you came here for Ellen, so don't try to deny it.

JOE. [*Sits settee down Left.*] I don't do things subconsciously! You're full of childish explanations of everything that comes up!

TOMMY. And you're full of psychological evasions!

ELLEN. [*Screaming.*] Oh, shut up! Both of you! I am not going to listen to any more of this! [*Runs upstairs.*]

[TOMMY *sits sofa up Center—there is a long pause.*]

JOE. Well I'll tell you one thing! I'm not going upstairs this time! [*Turns to* TOMMY.] If you'd explained what you were standing for on Saturday, things would have cleared up around here and I'd be in Washington now, talking to Ickes.

TOMMY. Are you still in love with Norma?

JOE. Norma who?

TOMMY. Your wife.

JOE. My wife's name is Brenda. And you're not going to talk her over with me. I can't be alone with you two minutes and have any private life left!

ELLEN'S VOICE. [*Off upstairs.*] Tommy! *What did you do with my nail file???!*

JOE. Oh, Lord—she sounds worse than last Saturday.

TOMMY. I haven't got it. [*He absently goes through a pocket, finds it, brings it out.*] Oh! Yeh, I've got it. [*He starts filing a nail.*]

JOE. I've gone through more hell here in three days than I've had with Phyllis in three years.

TOMMY. Yeh! [*Then he gets it; rising.*] Phyllis? Who is Phyllis? [*Crossing down to* JOE.] Are you carrying on with some other woman in Pittsburgh? You can't do this.

JOE. [*Springing to his feet.*] I'm not carrying on with anybody. Phyllis is my secretary and there's nothing between us!

TOMMY. Then why did you say you've been going through hell for three years?

JOE. [*Yelling.*] 'Cause you get me all balled up.

[ELLEN *comes downstairs with bag—sets it down Right.*]

TOMMY. [*Crossing to* ELLEN.] Here— [*Hands her nail file.*] You didn't pack anything!

ELLEN. [*Puts file in purse.*] I've been packed for three days! [*Crosses up Left; gets coat, puts it on; crosses Right to bag.*]

TOMMY. Well, you can't go with just one suitcase— There isn't much here, but—there're the books. They're yours. Most of them I gave to you. [*Turns away.*]

ELLEN. [*Putting on hat.*] Can I have "The Shropshire Lad"? [TOMMY *goes to Right bookcase; looks for book.*] Isn't that the one that has: [*Quotes.*]
    "And now the fancy passes by—"

TOMMY. [*Finds book; brings it to her.*]
    "And nothing will remain—"

MICHAEL. [*Sticks his head in door Left.*] You've just five minutes to get to your class, Mr. Turner. We'll wait for you in the car.

TOMMY. Thanks! [MICHAEL *exits, closing door. Crossing to* JOE.] Well, so long, Joe. I know you'll get Ellen a place of her own for a while anyway. [*Crossing to* EL-LEN.] Ellen can take that four-poster money with you. I'll have one more check coming, too. [*Starts upstairs.*]

JOE. What's "four-poster money"?

ELLEN. We were saving up to buy a new bed. [*Cries. Sits on Right settee.*]

JOE. Oh, my Lord, here we go again!

TOMMY. [*Crossing to* JOE.] Why did you have to ask what four-poster money is? [*Crossing to* ELLEN.] Ellen, please.

ELLEN. Oh, go on! Go on! Put on your coat and comb your hair! If you're going to be kicked out of school, you can't go over there looking like a tramp.

TOMMY. All right. [*Goes upstairs.*]

JOE. [*Pause.*] Look, Ellen, everything's gonna be all right. [*Crosses Center.*]

ELLEN. Is it?

JOE. [*Crossing up Left Center and looking upstairs.*] I wouldn't worry about that guy.

ELLEN. I don't.

JOE. I mean he's sure to get another job. He's had more publicity than Wally Myers.

ELLEN. I don't care what becomes of him.

JOE. [*Crosses to Center. Watches her for a moment.*] Come here. [*Crossing to her pulls her to her feet.*] You're still crazy about that guy, aren't you?

ELLEN. I'm kind of scared of him. He used to be just —nice, but now he's wonderful!

[TOMMY *appears on stairs in time to catch the end of this. Very slowly a light begins to dawn upon him.* JOE *sees him but* ELLEN *doesn't.*]

JOE. [*Looks around, sees Victrola, gets idea, pulls* ELLEN *across stage down Left to it.*] I don't think he's so wonderful!

[*WARN Curtain.*]

ELLEN. Yes, he is! That letter's wonderful. What he's trying to do is wonderful. He wouldn't let me or you or anyone stop him. Even Ed.

JOE. He's a scrapper all right, but he can't dance. [*Puts needle on.*]

[TOMMY *comes downstairs.* JOE *turns on Victrola which plays "Who."*]

ELLEN. Oh, who wants to dance now?

JOE. [*They are dancing.*] This is important. It's all in the light you give off.

ELLEN. [*He dances her Center.*] Light? What are you talking about?

JOE. The important thing about dancing is that the man has got to lead. [*Beckons to* TOMMY *who comes on into room from stairs.*]

TOMMY. [*Crossing to them.*] May I cut in? [*Takes* ELLEN *and dances with her.*]

ELLEN. Tommy! Let me go!

TOMMY. [*Shouting.*] No, I think you're wonderful too!

ELLEN. You think I'm dumb! Were you listening?

TOMMY. No.

JOE. [*Near door; out-yelling them.*] Hey—don't start that again!

TOMMY. [*Dancing upstage, gets his hat from table up Center and jams it on his head.*] Joe—why don't you go back to your wife? We can send her a wire.

JOE. Don't worry about me, Brother. I sent her a wire this morning. [*Goes out Left.*]

TOMMY. [*Dances with ELLEN.*] Quit leading!

ELLEN. I'm not leading. You *were* listening!

TOMMY. You were yelling. Well, turn!

ELLEN. [*At Center.*] Make me turn. [*He does and they turn, which brings them down Center. She finally breaks it.*] Don't be so rough—and put your hat on straight. [*She straightens his hat.*] You look terrible. [*She throws her arms around TOMMY and they kiss as—*

THE CURTAIN FALLS

COSTUME PLOT

ACT I

CLEOTA —gray dress uniform—green apron—(2) white apron

TOMMY —Brown tweed topcoat and hat, brown coat, gray pants; brown shoes,—dark gray suit, black shoes

ELLEN —short dress—turquoise blue, black shoes, brown tweed overcoat, brown hat, gloves, purse

PATRICIA —red shirt outside a plaid skirt, brown oxfords, brown dress, dubonnet shoes

WALLY —gray sweatshirt, leather jacket, brown pants, black shoes

DAMON —dark suit, coat, brown fedora hat, black shoes

MICHAEL —brown tweed suit, brown shoes, white sweater under coat

BLANCHE —brown overcoat black fur collar, short taffeta dress, white lace collar and cuffs, black shoes, black hat

JOE —dark blue suit, black shoes, heavy brown ulster, black derby

ED —light gray suit, black shoes, wrap-around overcoat, brown hat

MYRTLE —green velvet long gown, black fur collar, green slippers

NUTSY   —white pants, gold stripe, red West Point coat, shaker with red, white, blue plumes and red tassels

ACT II

Scene I

CLEOTA   —Green dress—green service apron

TOMMY   —Grey herringbone suit, black shoes, same topcoat and hat

ELLEN   —brown sport dress, brown shoes, plaid jacket, same overcoat and hat with orchid

PAT   —pink suit, brown light tan overcoat, brown hat, gloves, etc.

WALLY   —same

DAMON   —same

MIKE   —brown suit

ED   —brown tweed suit, brown soft hat, brown shoes

ACT II

Scene II

CLEOTA   —green dress, white apron

WALLY   —gray pants, red letter sweater, same jacket and shoes

CLEOTA   —green house dress, green apron

TOMMY   —terry cloth bathrobe and towel, bedroom slippers—same as Act II

ELLEN   —royal blue woolen dress; black shoes, same coat and accessories

PAT —same pink skirt with blue shirt

WALLY —gray pants, top coat (reversible), tie, letter sweater

MIKE —dark blue suit, black shoes, white sweater under coat

NUTSY —red turtle-neck sweater, corduroys, brown crepe soled shoes

REPORTER —gray coat, gray hat, gloves, black shoes

WORKING PROPERTY PLOT

ACT I

ONSTAGE

Straight chair down Right
Folding end table down Right
small book
nice ashtray (probably china)
small box wooden matches
Straight settee down Right
one brown cushion Left end
Long table back of settee
runner
lamp (bamboo base)
Continental telephone (dial)
large plate (painted green) concealed—to be broken
    in Act III
smaller ashtray
concealed matches
fairly large china vase filled with red and yellow pom-
    poms
Folding table up Right
1 full bottle sherry
1 full bottle vermouth
1 fairly large cocktail shaker (half full at rise)
1 tray with six cocktail glasses with toothpick and
    cherry in each glass
2 sherry glasses

1 small whiskey glass
1 bar towel
1 ashtray
Medium sized armchair down Right Center
Small end table up Right Center
   On Top
   cigarette box (patterned green china—cigarettes in-
      side)
   china ashtray
   china tobacco jar
   First Shelf
   three books
   Second Shelf
   three copies "Harper's" and one book
Long sofa up Center
two cushions (one dark green and one salmon)
Long table above sofa
three books Right end
lace runner
green cigarette box (cigarettes inside)
table lamp (brass metal base)
brown glass ashtray
one large green vase (empty—later holds chrysanthemums)
Straight chair up Left Center
Upholstered settee down Left
Two shelf coffee table below settee
   On top
   three copies "Harper's"
   glass ashtray
   brown wooden cigarette box (cigarettes and open
      box matches inside)
   Lower shelf

two books
Fireplace bench down Left
Radio-Victrola cabinet down Left
  On Top
  Radio-Victrola open with dummy record on table
  First Shelf
  pile of records, some with jackets
  Second Shelf
  pile of records, some with jackets
  Third Shelf
  four full albums of records
Andirons in fireplace
Fireplace set down Left
Waste-basket (metal) up Left
Waste-basket (cardboard) by table down Right
Bookcase on stairlanding
four shelves mixed books
  Dressing
  red pottery vase
  two books flat
  3 books standing
  china set of two zebras
Bookcase up Right Center
three shelves mixed books bottom shelf (4) Encyclo-
  pedia
  Dressing
  wooden cigarette box (cigarettes inside)
  tall pottery vase containing mixed pompoms
  two books flat
  two small packet pictures (one open standing—
    other flat)
Bookcase up Left
  Dressing

   green hexagonal vase containing a few roses
   two books flat

Bookcase Left
  Dressing
   books flat and standing (sets)
   one red glass vase
   two triangular metal ashtrays
   two china ornaments
   large metal vase with autumn leaves and pompoms
   five magazines, two books flat
four shelves of mixed books in both cases

Fireplace mantel Left
two crystal mantel lamps
one pair glass candlesticks
one china tobacco jar
one green china bowl
one tobacco pouch, three pipes

Window seat up Center
two cushions

Pictures
several pictures above stairs
two small flower prints above up Right Center bookcase
Pierrot-Pièrrette (Dégas) and print of Shakespeare
  above Left bookcase
still life above fireplace mantel
Dégas (solo dancer) above radio

Drapes
above down Right door
above window seat

Brackets
Upstage of down Right door
above up Right Center bookcase

Left of Center window
Hathooks up Left Center
Ellen's coat

OFF LEFT

wrapped bunch of chrysanthemums (wrapped in two sets of paper) flowers have rubber band around base of stems

two bottles scotch wrapped in paper and string

open copy of The Lit and folded English type umbrella

corsage box tied with string containing orchid

drum major's baton

newspaper with large picture of football player

wrapped bottle rum

several notebooks and one small textbook

small paper bag containing lb. of butter

two small pieces of adhesive tape

petition

OFF RIGHT

eight plates containing lettuce, celery, olives, pears, brown and wheat bread

large wooden cleanup tray

icebowl full of ice with ice tongs

tray of canapés

forks and napkins for eight plates

bakelite tray containing seven cups of coffee and sugar and creamer, spoons

three red sherbet glasses containing sherbet with spoons for each

green bakelite glass with spoon in it

two rum (old fashioned) glasses

hot water bottle and turkish towel

thermos bottle

two empty seltzer bottles

two highball glasses: one empty, one with inch of liquor

one almost empty Scotch bottle

one full Scotch bottle

one whiskey glass

small tray containing cup of tea, saucer and spoon

tray containing cup of coffee, two napkins, plate with knife and fork and bread, two glasses water, sugar bowl

three plates for offstage crash effects

book of Vanzetti letters

suitcase

orange crate and padded ironing board for special crash effects

box containing following for football setup
shaker, napkin, plate, fork
jampot, knife, shaker, spoon, cup, spoon, saucer
cup, knife, saucer, fork, shaker, knife, fork
creamer, plate, napkin, shaker

PERSONAL PROPS
clipping for WALLY
wristwatch for ED
wristwatch for MICHAEL
four small metal match-box covers and match-boxes inside for TOMMY
nail file for TOMMY
Turkish towel for TOMMY

ACT II

Scene I

Clear all plates from mantel, coffee table upstage table
    etc.
set football team on floor Center
set table down Right
move yellow chrysanthemums from up Center to up
    Right
move pompoms from down Right to up Center
cover bare spot on Left bookcase with magazines
turn off down Right light
JOE's hat and coat, ELLEN's and PAT's coats on coat-
    hooks
Center chair faces front
cigarette box from up Right Center bookcase to up
    Right table
empty waste-baskets
reverse cushions on both sofas
clear Right table of all liquor materials
open down Right door a little

ACT II

Scene 2

turn on down Right lamp
close down Right door
move up Right Center coffee table to upstage of settee
kill hot water bottle and towel
kill cream pitcher and glass up Center table
kill rum bottle, glass and newspaper coffee table

bring on seltzer bottles, highball glasses and empty
Scotch bottle to down Right table

ACT III

All furniture back to First Act marks
crash ashtray long table down Right
ELLEN's coat, TOMMY's coat and hat
green leaves Right table
kill chrysanthemums
pompoms to down Right table
books on fireplace bench to bookcase Left Center
kill roses up Left
close all doors
turn off down Right light
suitcase off upstairs

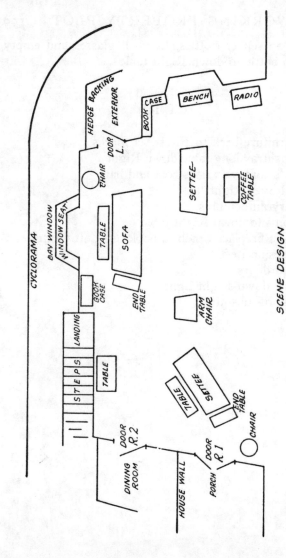

SCENE DESIGN

"THE MALE ANIMAL"